Developing healthy spiritual growth

'No one I know has a greater command of teaching practical godliness and experiential Christianity than Joel Beeke. Drawing upon Paul's prayer for the believers in Colossae, Beeke utilizes his exceptional exegetical abilities to lay open this text of Scripture, showing its primary relevance for the daily life of every believer. In so doing, this work will promote greater growth in grace and knowledge of Jesus Christ and deepen your spiritual life so that you may walk in a manner worthy of the Lord (Col. 1:10). This book should be a staple in your personal library regarding what constitutes genuine growth in biblical, reformed spirituality.'

Dr Steven J. Lawson
Senior Pastor, Christ Fellowship Baptist Church
Mobile, Alabama

'With his customary precision and clarity, Joel Beeke takes us through a remarkable study of what it means to grow spiritually. He shows that such growth is a fundamental element of the life of faith, and that it impacts every area of life. A careful reading of these Bible-saturated pages, full of practical wisdom and good counsel, will help God's people to live their lives before God's face, for the good of God's church, and in a Christ-glorifying manner.'

Iain D. Campbell
Minister of Point Free Church, Isle of Lewis, Scotland

'It is easy for Christians to be lopsided. Many stress doctrine at the expense of practice, and others pit experience against doctrine. *Developing Healthy Spiritual Growth* integrates growing in knowledge, practice, and experience into a biblically balanced and practical process of growing in grace. This book stands out by wedding doctrines such as communion with the Father, through the Son, by the Spirit, and the threefold office of Christ with Puritan-like application and heart-piercing and heart-warming expressions. This book will help you develop a well-rounded Christian life.'

Ryan McGraw
Pastor of First Orthodox Presbyterian Church
Sunnyvale, California

'My kids can't wait to grow taller. It's amusing to see them measure themselves painstakingly to detect the fractions of inches they may have grown in a few weeks, while refusing to eat the things that will help them grow. Combining knowledge of the Scriptures, the soul, and our spiritual heritage, Joel Beeke serves up a feast of growing foods. Better yet, here is a mouth-watering cookbook for all who would "grow in grace" (2 Peter 3:18).'

Dr Jerry Bilkes
Professor of New Testament
Puritan Reformed Theological Seminary, Grand Rapids, Michigan

Developing healthy spiritual growth

Knowledge, practice and experience

Joel R. Beeke

EP Books (Evangelical Press): Unit C, Tomlinson
Road, Leyland, PR25 2DY
epbooks@10ofthose.com
www.epbooks.org

First published 2013, reprinted 2016, 2019, 2021

British Library Cataloguing in Publication Data available
ISBN: 978-0-85234-947-2

Scripture quotations are from the Holy Bible, Authorized (King James) Version.

Contents

For this cause we also, since the day we heard it, do not cease to pray for you, and to desire that ye might be filled with the knowledge of his will in all wisdom and spiritual understanding; that ye might walk worthy of the Lord unto all pleasing, being fruitful in every good work, and increasing in the knowledge of God; strengthened with all might, according to his glorious power, unto all patience and longsuffering with joyfulness; giving thanks unto the Father, which hath made us meet to be partakers of the inheritance of the saints in light: who hath delivered us from the power of darkness, and hath translated us into the kingdom of his dear Son: in whom we have redemption through his blood, even the forgiveness of sins

(Colossians 1:9–14).

Preface

Biblical, Reformed spirituality and an accompanying need for personal spiritual growth has fallen on hard times. At a recent ministers' conference for the Free Reformed Churches in Ontario, I was asked to address the question of spiritual growth in terms of knowledge, practice and experience. I chose to do so using Colossians 1:9-14 as my background.

Since this book was originally given as addresses to ministers, I have retained some of the applications given directly to them. Those applications, however, are usually applicable to all believers in one way or another.

After the conference, some of the ministers present offered some valuable suggestions and asked me to publish these addresses. I am grateful for Graham Hind and Evangelical

Press's willingness to do so, and pray that God may use them to promote spiritual growth in his people.

Many thanks to Paul Smalley, Phyllis TenElshof, and Ray Lanning for their invaluable assistance on this manuscript. And, as always, many thanks to my remarkable wife, Mary, and dear children, for their generosity in allowing me the many hours that a writing ministry demands.

Joel R. Beeke

1
Spiritual growth in knowledge

For this cause we also, since the day we heard it, do not cease
to pray for you, and to desire that ye might be filled with the
knowledge of his will in all wisdom and spiritual understanding;
that ye might walk worthy of the Lord unto all pleasing,
being fruitful in every good work,
and increasing in the knowledge of God
(Colossians 1:9-10).

By today's standards, the ancient city of Colossae was a place of no great importance. Centuries before Christ, Colossae had been a large and flourishing center of commerce and textile manufacturing, located on the main highway running east to west through Phrygia. In Roman times, however, the highway was relocated to the north, leaving Colossae off the beaten path. Years of economic decline had reduced the city to a small town scraping by in the shadow of Laodicea, ten miles away. Around the time

Paul wrote to the Colossians, the area suffered a damaging earthquake. Accordingly, it might also be thought that a church planted in such unpromising circumstances would be of no great consequence or strategic importance in the larger context of the mission of the gospel to the Gentiles.[1]

But when we read Paul's epistle, we see things in a very different light. In Colossians 1, Paul celebrates the conversion of 'the saints and faithful brethren in Christ which are at Colossae' with heartfelt unceasing thanks to God. Paul was thrilled that 'the word of the truth of the gospel' had come to the Colossians through the faithful ministry of Epaphras, and was bearing much fruit. He thanked God for the new believers' faith in Christ and their love for 'all the saints', both of which were a gift from God and marks of his grace at work among them. Many members of the infant church at Colossae had been soundly converted, by the grace of God, leaving the darkness of their unbelieving past behind, and embracing the light of the gospel of Jesus Christ.

Clearly the particular circumstances of the church did not matter to Paul. The location of the church, and its temporal circumstances, were of no interest to him. He was not concerned about numbers or budgets or programs. What mattered was, the gospel was being preached, and the Lord Jesus was gathering his church in Colossae. God had honored his Word. God had used his faithful servant. A good foundation had been laid, and the Colossian believers had begun well. That is something to celebrate, something to give thanks to God for.

But Paul went on to say that he prayed constantly that what God had begun in the believers at Colossae would continue, and increase in depth and scope, filling them with the knowledge of God's will, inclining them and empowering them 'to walk worthy of the Lord unto all pleasing', more and more. Paul rejoiced in the beginning they had made, but he also longed for spiritual growth. So should we.

What is spiritual growth? Spiritual growth is the development of the believer's faith and life in learning to know, trust and honor the Triune God intellectually and experientially, which issues in the Spirit's graces exercised in conformity to Christ through practical Christian living. By this growth a deeper insight is also gained into spiritual liberty.

There is a saying: 'The biggest room in the world is the room for improvement.'[2] Certainly that is true of our spiritual lives. We must not be satisfied to say that we have been born again, but pray that the child of our new birth would grow into a mature man. Spiritual growth should be as natural to believers as physical growth is to children. Regardless of the number of people involved, or the social or strategic importance of the church, God's will for all his children is that they grow up to maturity in Christ.

Wilhelmus á Brakel provides several reasons spiritual growth should be a staple part of every believer's life: first, 'God promises that He will cause His regenerated children to grow' (Ps. 92:13; Hosea 14:5-6; Mal. 4:2); second, 'it is the very nature of spiritual life to grow' (Prov. 4:18; Job 17:9); third, 'the growth of His children is the goal and objective God has in view by administering the means of grace to them' (Eph. 4:11-15; 1 Peter 2:2); fourth, 'it is a duty to which God's children are continually exhorted, and their activity is to consist in a striving for growth' (2 Peter 3:18; Phil. 3:12); and finally, the need for spiritual growth 'is also conveyed by the difference in believers in regard to their condition and the measure of grace' (1 John 2:13).[3]

Such spiritual growth vindicates a believer's claims to have been converted. Regeneration creates new desires. As Matthew 5:6 says, 'Blessed are they which do hunger and thirst after righteousness.' Such persons are blessed because they have been begotten again unto new life in Christ. A healthy infant has a strong appetite, and the newborn child of God wants more of God. Lack of appetite in a child is a symptom of sickness. Lack of spiritual appetite in a professing Christian is a very disturbing sign. Gardiner Spring (1785-1873) said, 'The hypocrite, when once he imagines himself to be a Christian, views his work as done. He is satisfied. He is rich and increased in goods. But it is otherwise with the true Christian... The more he loves God, the more he desires to love Him.'[4]

So Paul prayed for the new converts at Colossae. He provides a detailed summary of his prayers, giving us a description of true spiritual growth. Let us soak our minds and hearts in the rich broth of this passage of Holy Scripture so that we may know what true spiritual growth is, and how it takes place. Then let us climb this text as a high hill from which to survey the broader biblical teaching on growing in grace.

Before getting into the details, let us observe something we may otherwise overlook. All spiritual growth ultimately comes from the Holy Spirit. Why else would Paul pray for such growth, if God did not give it? Paul wrote in 1 Corinthians 3:6: 'I have planted, Apollos watered; but God gave the increase.' Just as we must thank God for our conversion, so we must also pray for spiritual growth from his hands. Indeed, Paul by example teaches us that praying for spiritual growth should be a high priority for us. We are told that Paul and his co-workers did not cease to pray for this growth. It was their constant prayer for the 'saints and faithful brethren' of the Colossian church. We see this same priority in Paul's other letters: constant prayer for the spiritual growth of all Christians, and the churches they belong to.[5]

Do you pray for spiritual growth in yourself and in the church? Is it your priority? It will do us little good to talk about spiritual growth if you do not yearn for it and pray for it. Robert Rollock (1555-1598) said, 'Earnest and fervent prayer to God is the means to get grace from him.'[6] If we do not want to fall under the rebuke of James 4:2: 'Ye have not, because ye ask not', we must pray for ourselves, our families, our fellow believers, and our churches. Notice that the church at Colossae was not one that Paul planted, for which he was personally responsible. This church was planted by Epaphras, perhaps with the assistance of Archippus (4:17). But even so, these Christians were dear to Paul, and he prayed for them as lovingly and faithfully as for any other. As you pray for the church you serve, do you also pray for other churches in your communities? Do you pray for churches in other places? Let us offer prayers that walk all over the globe for the sake of God's church!

Taking up the contents of Paul's prayer, we learn that spiritual growth is like a diamond; it has many facets. It begins in the head and the heart (v. 9), works itself out in our daily lives (vv. 10, 11), and is consummated in the praise and thanksgiving that we offer by word and deed to our Father in heaven (v. 12) for our deliverance in Christ (v. 13). Peter presents the matter in even more detail: 'And beside this, giving all diligence, add to your faith virtue; and to virtue knowledge; and to knowledge temperance; and to temperance patience; and to patience godliness; and to godliness brotherly kindness; and to brotherly kindness charity' (2 Peter 1:5-7). Spiritual growth is part of the larger doctrine of sanctification, involving the exposition of the requirements of the law, and the use of the means of grace. To stay within the bounds of the subjects allotted to me, therefore, we need to be focused and succinct in our examination of spiritual growth.

This book will thus consist of how to grow spiritually in knowledge, practice and experience. All three are suggested in our text. In his prayer, Paul first pleaded for believers' growth in knowledge: 'that ye might be filled with the knowledge of his will in all wisdom and spiritual understanding'. Knowledge is primary in spiritual growth, and everything else flows from it. After this request, Paul said, 'that ye might walk worthy of the Lord unto all pleasing', which explains the purpose of being filled with knowledge. Growth in practice flows out of growth in knowledge. This worthy walk is then qualified by four Greek participles: 'being fruitful', 'increasing', being 'strengthened', and 'giving thanks'. The first two participles reiterate the ideas of growth in practice and knowledge, but the second two add another quality: growth in experience. So here are all three elements of our topic.

Let us focus first on the theme of spiritual growth as growth in knowledge. We will first examine Paul's foundational prayer request in verse 9, and the phrase in verse 10 about 'increasing in the knowledge of God'.

Like so many writings of Paul, this prayer reflects the Trinitarian structure of God's saving work. It is not as plain as in Paul's prayers in Ephesians, but just below the surface of his words, we quickly discover that the Father,

Son and Holy Spirit are both the source and the goal of our spiritual growth. This suggests a threefold structure to our consideration of spiritual growth in knowledge: growth in knowledge of the Son, of the Father, and of the Holy Spirit.

Grow in knowledge of the Son

Colossians 1:9 says that Paul constantly prayed 'that ye might be filled with the knowledge of his will'. 'His will' means the will of the Lord Jesus Christ, whom Paul first mentions in verse 3: 'We give thanks to God and the Father of our Lord Jesus Christ'. The will in this case is particularly the revealed will of the Lord Jesus, as confirmed in verse 10. Such a description is consistent with the terms of the Great Commission. Preachers of the gospel are to make disciples of all nations, 'teaching them to observe all things whatsoever I have commanded you' (Matt. 28:19-20).

Being filled with Christ's will

Paul's words 'be filled' also point to Christ. Filling and fullness is a major theme in this epistle, which declares the overflowing sufficiency of Christ.[7] Colossians 1:19 says, 'For it pleased the Father that in him should all fulness dwell.' Colossians 2:9-10 relates Christ's fullness to our being filled or completed: 'For in him dwelleth all the fulness of the Godhead bodily. And ye are complete in him, which is the head of all principality and power.' About this Rollock wrote: 'God is full. O what fullness is in God! Jesus Christ is full … then it must follow … we must be filled with that fullness of God.'[8] So Paul's language to 'be filled' evokes the idea of going to Christ as the infinite and inexhaustible treasury of blessing to receive more and more of his grace.

Being filled increasingly with knowledge

We must seek grace to be filled increasingly with knowledge. Paul was satisfied that the Colossians understood the basics of the gospel, but he did not want them to stop there. In their zeal and enthusiasm to serve their new Lord, they should not forget to sit at his feet and learn from him as true disciples. John Angell James wrote: 'Young converts are sometimes so taken up with religious feeling and doing, as to forget the importance, even in reference to these, of knowing.'[9]

Sanctifying knowledge

Being filled with such knowledge is more than just acquiring an education, however. If such knowledge were only a matter of education, truth would only be present in the intellect and would not fill one's entire being. To be filled with knowledge means that these truths permeate one's mind, heart and life as the fragrance of brewing coffee fills a house in the morning. We must keep God's truths percolating in us until they flavor all that we are in Christ.

Thus the whole person is involved in sanctifying knowledge. The mind, which possesses an understanding darkened by sin; the emotions and feelings, which are permeated with distorted affections; and the will, which is not free by nature — all must be renovated by sanctified knowledge. By grace, the Holy Spirit enlightens the believer's mind, cleanses his feelings, and renews his will. Since all three are interconnected, a sanctified understanding leads to sanctified feelings, which in turn impacts the will.

Bible commentator Curtis Vaughan writes: 'To be "filled" with the knowledge of the divine will suggests that such knowledge is to pervade all of one's being — thoughts, affections, purposes, and plans.'[10] Colossians 3:16-17 says, 'Let the word of Christ dwell in you richly in all wisdom; teaching and admonishing one another in psalms and hymns and spiritual songs, singing with grace in your hearts to the Lord. And whatsoever ye do in word or deed, do all in the name of the Lord Jesus, giving thanks to God and the Father by him.'

Growing spiritual knowledge will consist of:

1. *A growing understanding of God's holy law.* In saying we are to be 'filled with the knowledge of *his will'*, Paul was

saying our sanctification is an important part of God's will (1 Thess. 4:3) and that we must be 'doing the will of God from the heart' (Eph. 6:6). So part of what Paul prayed for here is a deeper understanding of God's *holy law*. Psalm 119:33-34 says, 'Teach me, O LORD, the way of thy statutes; and I shall keep it unto the end. Give me understanding, and I shall keep thy law; yea, I shall observe it with my whole heart.'

Knowing God's will in its holiness humbles us, for by the law we know our sin (Rom. 3:20). As we sink downward in penitence and brokenness, we grow closer to God. Isaiah 57:15 says, 'For thus saith the high and lofty One that inhabiteth eternity, whose name is Holy; I dwell in the high and holy place, with him also that is of a contrite and humble spirit, to revive the spirit of the humble, and to revive the heart of the contrite ones.'

2. A growing understanding of God's holy gospel. God's will is also the *holy gospel*. God's will is his sovereign plan of salvation in Christ, which includes justification but is far more than that. Notice that in verse 6 Paul thanked God that the Colossian believers 'knew the grace of God in truth'. They knew God as their Savior in Christ. Then he prays for them to be filled with the knowledge of God as their Sanctifier in Christ. This view of God's will is consistent with Paul's references to the divine will in Ephesians 1, which says that God predestined people to salvation in Christ 'according to the good pleasure of his will' (v. 5), and 'made known unto us the mystery of his will' (v. 9), for he is the God 'who worketh all things after the counsel of his own will' (v. 11). In other words, Paul prays for deeper knowledge of God's total plan of redemption in the person and work of his Son. He is the One who came into the world crying, 'Lo, I come … to do thy will, O God' (Heb. 10:7). Therefore God's will is not merely what God wants us to do; it is also what God has done, is doing and will do through his Son.

Paul's prayer that we would be filled with the knowledge of God's purposes in Christ is consistent with the words of Peter's salutation in 2 Peter 1:2-4: 'Grace and peace be multiplied unto you through the knowledge of God, and of Jesus our Lord, according as his divine power hath given unto us all things that pertain unto life and godliness, through the knowledge of him that hath called us to glory and virtue: whereby are given unto us exceeding great and precious promises: that by these ye might be partakers of the divine nature, having escaped the corruption that is in the world through lust.' God's grace and peace are multiplied to us through the knowledge of God and Christ. This knowledge is sufficient for all things that pertain to life and godliness. This knowledge is summed up in his precious promises.

3. A growing Christ-centered knowledge. The knowledge we need is centered in the Mediator. If we would be filled with this knowledge, we must sit at the feet of Christ, and learn of him. Christ 'is ordained of God the Father, and anointed with the Holy Ghost, to be our chief Prophet and Teacher, who has fully revealed to us the secret counsel and will of God concerning our redemption'.[11] He is also the wisdom of God, for 'in [him] are hid all the treasures of wisdom and knowledge' (Col. 2:3; *cf.* Prov. 8 and 9). Christ is both the Messenger and the Message of salvation. Note that after Paul prays for increasing knowledge, he gives us a brilliant exposition of the riches of Christ and how we make use of them. He was thus praying that God would open up his treasure-chest, his Son Jesus Christ, and fill us with the gold and silver of his truth. Likewise, Peter summed up all Christian growth by saying, 'But grow in grace, and in the knowledge of our Lord and Savior Jesus Christ. To him be glory both now and for ever. Amen' (2 Peter 3:18).

Matthew Henry said, 'Spiritual growth consists most in the growth of the root, which is out of sight. The more we depend upon Christ and draw sap and virtue from him … the more we cast forth our roots.'[12] In other words, the deeper our roots are in Christ, the more we will grow in communion with him. Colossians 2:6-7 says, 'As ye have therefore received Christ Jesus the Lord, so walk ye in him: rooted and built up in him.'

Spiritual growth begins with knowledge. We must be increasingly filled with the knowledge of Christ as the Agent of the Father's will. If our spiritual life is a fire burning in our hearts, then doctrinal truth received by grace is the well-seasoned wood that fuels the fire, so that it burns hotter and higher. O that God would make our churches great bonfires that blaze in the night of this dark world!

Useful knowledge

Let me suggest some implications that follow from this truth.

1. *It gives us a mandate for Christian education in home, church and school.* If spiritual growth begins with being filled with the knowledge of Christ, then the result of neglecting Christian education will be malnourished, stunted, underdeveloped Christians. Zeal for God without knowledge is deadly, says Romans 10:2. John Davenant (1572-1641) wrote: 'A blind ignorance, however devoted, is not pleasing to God.'[13] But a well-catechized people have the foundations for vibrant spiritual growth.

Certainly we must read our Bibles to grow spiritually. Psalm 1 reminds us that God's blessing rests upon the person who meditates with delight, day and night, on the law of the Lord. One great heritage of the Reformation is the translation of the Bible into the language of the people, and the right of people to read it for themselves. It was good for the Ethiopian eunuch to read aloud from

Isaiah 53 in his chariot. But when Philip asked the man if he understood what he was reading, the eunuch honestly replied: 'How can I, except some man should guide me?' (Acts 8:30-31). People need guidance in understanding biblical doctrine. Ephesians 4:11-13 tells us that Christ gave pastors and teachers to build up the body, 'till we all come in the unity of the faith, and of the knowledge of the Son of God, unto a perfect man'.

The Reformed churches have a strong heritage of teaching the truth. But the winds of culture blow through our ranks, and the undertow of the world's tide often sucks us out to sea. We all want to be popular and admired by others. Who wants to look like an intolerant, narrow-minded bigot? But absolute, uncompromising truth is the meat and drink of a true Christian and a faithful church. Never back down from teaching people the truth of the Bible.

2. *This calls for an insatiable hunger to learn more of God's truth.* Paul's prayer is that we would be 'filled' with knowledge. He does not pray for a drip here and a drip there of knowledge, but for a torrent like Niagara Falls. No Christian will ever know enough of God's truth. Men who graduate from seminary must remember that they have not yet graduated from the school of Christ. Ministers in particular must be reading, studying, listening and learning throughout their life. John Calvin (1509-1564) said, 'We must always make progress in the doctrine of piety until death.'[14]

Christians must study the Holy Scriptures. First Peter 2:2 tells us: 'As newborn babes, desire the sincere milk of the word, that ye may grow thereby.' Notice that Peter did not say, 'You who are newborn babes in the faith, do this.' He called all believers 'newborn babes', indicating that we all need to grow up. None of us will reach complete spiritual maturity until Christ's return (1 Cor. 13:10-12). Our goal till then must be always to seek maturity in Christ (Eph. 4:13).

So let the Word of Christ dwell in you richly. Do not lean on old studies and favorite verses, which, like bread, go stale. Get your manna fresh each day. Explore the Bible as a prince exploring the property he has inherited from his royal father. Meditate on the Scriptures by turning over a single verse at a time in your mind and savoring its teaching. Review and restudy familiar parts of Scripture, and press on into parts you have neglected until now. Feed yourself before you feed your flock.

3. *This places Christ at the center of the cultivation of a Christian mind.* Bible doctrine is a ring designed to hold a single, sparkling diamond: Jesus Christ. Paul says in 1 Corinthians 2:2, 'For I determined not to know any thing among you, save Jesus Christ, and him crucified.' But Paul, will you not teach us about the church? Yes, but only as the body of Christ. We can learn about a wife's submission to her husband as her head and she should express that publicly,

but only in the context of our common submission to Christ, our head.

Remember that 'it pleased the Father that in him should all fullness dwell'. The Father's desire and delight is that all of our thinking and teaching be centered in his Son, Jesus. God does not want his Son ever to be taken for granted because he loves his Son with an infinite love. So the Father is displeased with any teaching or thinking that marginalizes Christ. Christ must be central in all things. John Owen (1616-1683) said, 'If I have observed anything by experience it is this — a man may take the measure of his growth and decay in grace according to his thoughts and meditations upon the person of Christ and the glory of Christ's kingdom and of his love.'[15]

Growing in the knowledge of Christ is central for spiritual growth and grounds us in grace. It is so natural to try to build our spiritual growth upon self-righteousness and self-effort. Robert Murray M'Cheyne (1813-1843) said, 'Many look to a wrong quarter for sanctification. They take pardon from Christ, then lean on themselves ... for holiness. Ah, no; you must take hold of the hand that was pierced.'[16]

Jerry Bridges says, 'A correct understanding of God's grace and a consistent appropriation of it must be the foundation of all our personal efforts to grow spiritually.'[17]

He says two bookends must be in place or all our 'books', or efforts to grow spiritually, will fall down. One bookend is Christ's righteousness as our only ground of acceptance with God. The other is Christ's power as our only source of ability to become holy. By constantly studying Christ, we will cultivate dependence upon God's grace.[18]

Pursue the knowledge of Christ for your own mind and soul. Read Scripture with an eye to Christ. Read the best treatises on the doctrine of Christ: Thomas Goodwin's *Christ our Mediator,* Isaac Ambrose's *Looking unto Jesus,* Ralph Robinson's *Christ All and in All,* Philip Henry's book also titled, *Christ All in All,* John Brown's *Christ: The Way, the Truth, and the Life,* John Owen's *The Glorious Mystery of the Person of Christ,* and James Durham's *Christ Crucified.*[19]

Christ is the consolation of the church. Our only comfort, according to the *Heidelberg Confession*, is that we 'belong unto our faithful Savior Jesus Christ'.[20] Christless preaching is comfortless preaching. Those of us who are ministers must examine our preaching. What has your congregation learned in the last few months about the Mediator and his natures, states and offices? Have they come to see the beauty of his great heart more clearly and to feel it more dearly? What have you brought them from the Word to show how Christ rules his church through various commandments and propels the church forward in its mission?

Is Christ crucified and risen a magnet that attracts all of your instruction? Or is he becoming marginal, perhaps even forgotten? This will not help believers grow in maturity. Paul says in Ephesians 4:13 that the goal of ministry is that 'we all come in the unity of the faith, and of the knowledge of the Son of God'. Spiritual growth begins with being filled with the knowledge of Christ as the Agent of his Father's will. Therefore, seek grace to grow in knowledge of the Son.

Grow in knowledge of the Holy Spirit

Note that Paul goes on in verse 9 to pray for believers to be filled with the knowledge of God's saving will in Christ 'in all wisdom and spiritual understanding'. By speaking of 'spiritual understanding' Paul distinguishes it from the knowledge that is ordinarily accessible to fallen men. Paul uses the word *spiritual* here, as almost everywhere else, as that which belongs to or comes from the Holy Spirit.

Spiritual knowledge imparted by the Spirit

'Spiritual understanding' is knowledge imparted to us by the illumination of the Spirit. And whatever comes from the Holy Spirit is characterized by his holiness.

First Corinthians 2:11-16 makes it plain that we must depend on the Holy Spirit to have true knowledge of God: 'What man knoweth the things of a man, save the spirit of man which is in him? Even so the things of God knoweth no man, but the Spirit of God. Now we have received, not the spirit of the world, but the spirit which is of God; that we might know the things that are freely given to us of God. Which things also we speak, not in the words which man's wisdom teacheth, but which the Holy Ghost teacheth; comparing spiritual things with spiritual. But the natural man receiveth not the things of the Spirit of God: for they are foolishness unto him: neither can he know them, because they are spiritually discerned. But he that is spiritual judgeth all things, yet he himself is judged of no man. For who hath known the mind of the Lord, that he may instruct him? But we have the mind of Christ.'

The Spirit opened our eyes in conversion, but now we must seek his light to shine more and more, to expand our spiritual vision of all God's blessings in Christ. Paul also prayed for this in Ephesians 1:17-18, saying, 'That the God of our Lord Jesus Christ, the Father of glory, may give unto you the spirit of wisdom and revelation in the knowledge of him: the eyes of your understanding being enlightened.' John Eadie (1810-1876) observed: 'This enjoyment of the Spirit of Light is the special privilege of believers. He dispels the mists which obscure the inner vision, [and] fills the soul with an ardent relish for Divine truth and a fuller perception of it.'[21]

Christ-minded knowledge

Paul called such spiritual knowledge 'having the mind of Christ'. It is more than information; it is also 'wisdom'. The mind of Christ is the mind of a humble servant (Phil. 2:5-8). Spiritual knowledge is a Spirit-indwelt, Spirit-imparted mindset; an experience of life and peace, found in submission to God's law, and belonging to Christ (Rom. 8:6-9). 'The law is spiritual' (Rom. 7:14), breathed out by God, and imbued with the life and holiness of God's Spirit (2 Tim. 3:16-17). It is 'the spirit of … the fear of the LORD', who anoints men to delight in the fear of the Lord (Isa. 11:2-3).

Vital, transforming knowledge

Therefore Paul did not pray for mere mental knowledge but for the vital, transforming knowledge given by the Holy Spirit. Calvin wrote: 'Indeed we shall not say that, properly speaking, God is known where there is not religion or piety … I call "piety" that reverence joined with love of God which the knowledge of his benefits induces.'[22] We must realize that in dividing the topic of spiritual growth into knowledge, practice and experience, we are setting up artificial divisions for the sake of clarity. In reality these things are inseparable.

Active knowledge

Colossians 1:9-10 indicates that spiritual knowledge produces spiritual conduct, activity and behavior: 'that ye might be filled with the knowledge of his will in all wisdom and spiritual understanding; that ye might walk worthy of the Lord'. A worthy walk is the purpose of the person who is filled with knowledge.[23] Paul said in 1 Timothy 1:5: 'Now the end [or goal] of the commandment is charity out of a pure heart, and of a good conscience, and of faith unfeigned.' Sinclair Ferguson says, 'The goal of theology is the worship of God. The posture of theology is on one's knees. The mode of theology is repentance.'[24]

Humbling knowledge

This kind of knowledge should humble us. Anne Dutton (1692-1765) wrote: 'As to my knowledge of divine truths, I find it very small: especially if it be reduced to that which is practical; or to that knowledge which influences the soul into an answerable practice. I am entirely of your mind, "that our refreshment in truths, depends upon the Spirit's breathing…" If the Spirit shines upon old-known truths, we behold them in a new glory; and if he breathes in them afresh upon our souls, we're filled with new life immediately.'[25]

Knowledge often produces nothing but an over-inflated ego (1 Cor. 8:1). Paul did not pray for that kind of knowledge, for ego inflation is the very opposite of spiritual growth. Such wisdom is 'earthly, sensual, devilish', and promoted 'envy and strife' (James 3:15-16). This kind of knowledge, which has no connection with the Spirit, is what gives doctrine a bad name.

Loving knowledge

What makes spiritual understanding different from dead orthodoxy? Spiritual knowledge energizes the heart with love, the great fruit of the Spirit (Gal. 5:22). Paul told the Colossians in verse 8 that the truth of the gospel produces the fruit of 'love in the Spirit'. He prayed in Philippians 1:9: 'that your love may abound yet more and more in knowledge'. Spiritual understanding touches the mind but also the heart, the will and the affections with the loveliness of God, his ways, and his image in man. The only way to know God is to love him humbly (1 Cor. 8:1-3). In humility we seek to know him as he is in himself. D. Martyn Lloyd-Jones said, 'There is no better test of growth than that a man desires God because he is God.'[26]

Digested knowledge

Picture two men with a pizza. One man has a stomach ulcer and cannot eat pizza, but he is a biochemist with a detailed knowledge of the composition of pizza and and how its ingredients are combined and processed to produce the final product. The other man may know little about what is in it, or how it is made, but he wants to eat it, and thoroughly enjoys it. This is analogous to spiritual knowledge: the believer 'tastes and sees' that the Lord is good, and therefore loves him, loves his Word, and loves his image in men (1 Peter 2:1-3). Growth in spiritual knowledge is not so much a matter of mere quantity of information, but of quality of understanding, a taste of the heart that relishes the gifts and goodness and glory of God. Therefore we must not aim merely to grow in the knowledge of God's will in his Son, but also to grow in spiritual understanding of this truth.

Useful knowledge

What does this imply for our lives and ministries?

1. *We should study, teach and pray, relying on the Holy Spirit's help.* Paul was a master preacher, pastor, teacher and theologian. But he knew he would be a fool if he just taught and wrote. He also had to pray. He prayed for God to fill believers with 'spiritual understanding', for otherwise, all his teaching and writing would be in vain. He understood that without the Spirit indwelling and working in the heart, no one could even say for his own soul, 'Jesus is the Lord' (1 Cor. 12:3). Prayer is the special duty of ministers for their people. Paul Baynes (*c*. 1573–1617) said, 'Ministers must not only teach and admonish, but pray for their people.'[27] Samuel said in 1 Samuel 12:23:

'Moreover as for me, God forbid that I should sin against the LORD in ceasing to pray for you: but I will teach you the good and the right way.'

Christ taught believers to pray for the Holy Spirit as children ask their father for food (Luke 11:11-13). Paul prayed that the Father would give the Ephesian believers 'the spirit of wisdom and revelation' to enlighten their hearts in the knowledge of God (Eph. 1:17-18). Without the Spirit we are only the blind leading the blind. Pray for the Spirit every time you open the Bible, brothers, and pray again for Spirit-given understanding before you close it.

2. *We should beware of unspiritual knowledge.* We could spend hours filling our brains with the details of the text of Scripture, but without love, we would be useless as God's messengers (1 Cor. 13:2). We would be worse than useless, because such unspiritual knowledge destroys individuals, families and churches while waving the banner of theological purity.

Unspiritual knowledge, that is, knowledge without Christ, without the Spirit, without love for God and men, is not 'halfway to the mark' but entirely opposed to God. It is hypocrisy, outwardly maintaining the doctrines of Scripture while inwardly opposing the God of Scripture. With unspiritual knowledge men use God for their own purposes; they subordinate God's revelation to self-love, which is a blasphemous reversal.

'Who is a wise man and endued with knowledge among you? Let him shew out of a good conversation his works with meekness of wisdom. But if ye have bitter envying and strife in your hearts, glory not, and lie not against the truth' (James 3:13-14). We must judge our knowledge by its fruits in our lives. A good understanding leads to a good application. Spiritual truth produces spiritual fruit. If we lack these things, our boasting should be replaced with repentance.

3. *We should preach and teach with much love.* To light a fire, you must first strike a match. God does not need to work through means, and certainly not through sinful men, such as we are, but thankfully he chooses to do so. If we want the Lord to use us to impart spiritual knowledge to others, we ourselves must first have that knowledge burning in our minds, and filling our hearts with love.

Paul wrote in 1 Thessalonians 1:5: 'Our gospel came not unto you in word only, but also in power, and in the Holy Ghost, and in much assurance; as ye know what manner of men we were among you for your sake.' To preach the gospel in power and in the Spirit, we must be a certain 'manner of men', who are as nurses who cherish their children, and fathers who exhort and comfort them (1 Thess. 2:7-12).

Spiritual growth begins with growth in the knowledge of Christ as the Agent of his Father's will. This is not the knowledge available to fallen men, to be acquired by their own efforts, but the spiritual understanding that the Holy Spirit imparts and uses to energize us with love. Therefore we need to grow in the knowledge of the Son communicated by the Spirit.

Grow in knowledge of the Father

In Colossians 1:10 Paul writes that his goal when praying for Christians to be filled by the Spirit with the knowledge of the Son was that they would also increase in 'the knowledge of God'. Why does he say that? Hasn't he just said in verse 9 that he was praying for them to be filled with knowledge? This is not mere repetition for emphasis; rather, as we noted before, the structure of the text suggests that 'increasing in the knowledge of God' is one of the purposes of being 'filled with the knowledge of his will'.

Knowledge affirming the Trinity

Ordinarily Paul uses the word *God* for the Father and *Lord* for the Son.[28] So most likely Paul was thinking here of God the Father in praying that believers increase 'in the knowledge of God'. This makes sense, for Paul has already prayed for believers to be filled with the knowledge of Christ's will for their lives. He has already spoken of knowledge by the Spirit. If they know the Son through the Holy Spirit, they will see, as Paul says in verse 15, that Christ 'is the image of the invisible God'. To know Christ is also to know the Father reflected in him.

The great goal of the new covenant is that human beings should know the Father, through the Son, by the Holy Spirit. In the lively preaching of the Word, the Holy Spirit opens our minds and illumines our hearts with 'the light of the knowledge of the glory of God in the face of Christ', and are transformed by becoming conformed to the glorious person of Christ (2 Cor. 4:4,6). In Christ we see God the Father in a way that gives life to our souls. Because the fullness of God dwells bodily, in Christ, the true nature of the Father is revealed through the Son. This is the promise of the new covenant in Jeremiah 31:34: 'They shall all know me.' This is the goal of our earthly pilgrimage, for each step along the way brings us into deeper knowledge of God as our Father.

Knowledge affirming the riches of God's love

O the riches of the love of God, that he would send his Son to the cross for sinners, and pour his Spirit into our hearts, so that we could know his love! What depths of wonder and joy lie in those simple words, 'Grace be unto you, and peace, from God our Father and the Lord Jesus Christ' (Col. 1:2). Can this be true? Yes, it is true of everyone in whom God plants faith and love through the gospel. Our spiritual growth includes coming to know the eternal God who is now, for the sake of Christ his Son, our God and Father.

Useful knowledge

Let us consider the implications for our lives.

1. *We should seek grace to grow in the knowledge of our adoption.* We must not neglect to teach the doctrine of adoption alongside the doctrines of election and justification. Adoption is not merely a step or gateway through which we pass when we are saved. It is rather part of the great purpose of God in redemption. Just as God elected us to holiness, so he predestined us 'unto the adoption of children by Jesus Christ to himself' (Eph. 1:4-5), 'that he might be the firstborn among many brethren' (Rom. 8:29). 'Beloved, now are we the sons of God' (1 John 3:2).

As believers, we need to grow in our understanding of God's fatherly heart, his loving purposes towards us, and his faithful dealings with us. We must teach this precious doctrine not as a mere item in the plan of salvation, but as God's benediction on the whole of our lives, including our prayer lives as God's children, our sanctification as God's children, our sufferings as God's children, and our ultimate hope as God's children.

As I stated in my book *Heirs with Christ,* there are many benefits to adoption, and we should grow in our appreciation and appropriation of them.[29] Our Father calls us out of the mass of fallen humanity, and brings us into his family. We are called by his name, given access to the throne of grace, experience his love, and enjoy the liberty and privileges of his children and heirs, to whom he has given exceeding great and precious promises of protection, provision and preservation. All this has been secured to us by the shedding of the blood of Christ, and all of this is revealed and confirmed to us by the Spirit as the Spirit of adoption.

Our Father comforts us with his love and pity. He moves us to rejoice in intimate communion with him and his Son. Through his Spirit, he assists us in performing spiritual duties. He counsels and directs us. He chastens and corrects us. Our Father preserves us and keeps us from falling. He provides everything we need as his children. He sends forth his angels as ministering spirits to serve us. He makes our death 'an abolishing of sin and a passage into eternal life'.[30] Is any part of our existence left untouched by the fatherhood of God to his adopted children? Then let us study and teach adoption.

2. *We should teach the biblical doctrine of God.* God has a wondrous simplicity in himself, but he has revealed his nature in a variety of attributes, much like white light that is separated by a prism into a rainbow of beautiful colors.

He does this for our edification, since one dimension of our spiritual growth is 'increasing in the knowledge of God'.

Defects in our knowledge of God produce systematic errors in our faith, obedience and worship. Jesus rebuked the Sadducees for denying the resurrection, saying, 'Ye do err, not knowing the scriptures, nor the power of God' (Matt. 22:29). If they knew God better, they would not have fallen into such heresies. Paul wrote in 1 Thessalonians 4:5 that we must abstain from fornication, and learn how to maintain sexual purity, as contrasted with 'the lust of concupiscence' so prevalent among 'the Gentiles which know not God'. As the Galatians were falling under the spell of Jewish legalism and man-made traditions, Paul reminded them, that 'when ye knew not God, ye did service unto them which by nature are no gods ... But now, after that ye have known God, or rather are known of God, how turn ye again to the weak and beggarly elements, whereunto ye desire again to be in bondage?' (Gal. 4:8-9). The knowledge of God is the best protection against error, heresy and superstition. John Eadie wrote: 'A God in shadow creates superstition.'[31]

Therefore believers must study God's attributes. On a basic level our children and adults should be familiar with the ABCs of God's nature. The *Belgic Confession* summarizes the faith of the church in its first article, which says, 'We all believe with the heart, and confess with the mouth, that there is one only simple and spiritual Being, which we call God; and that He is eternal, incomprehensible, invisible, immutable, infinite, almighty, perfectly wise, just, good, and the overflowing fountain of all good.'[32] Our goal should be to impart to all church members a basic understanding of these attributes, giving substance to the faith they confess, and the light of knowledge to lead them into closer communion with our God.

We should not be satisfied with knowing the basics, however. Each one of God's attributes is an opening into an underground mine that has walls loaded with diamonds and shafts that penetrate into endless depths. We must go deeper in the knowledge of God. This is especially true of pastors and teachers who are called to instruct others. Proverbs 9:10 says, 'The fear of the LORD is the beginning of wisdom: and the knowledge of the holy is understanding.' By the Spirit's grace, let us press on to know the Holy One better!

One way to do this is to make use of the good books God has provided. On the attributes of God, read the all-time classic, Stephen Charnock's *The Existence and Attributes of God,* or William Bates on *The Harmony of the Divine Attributes in … Redemption*. On the doctrine of the Trinity, see Edward Bickersteth on *The Trinity,* and more recently Robert Letham's *The Holy Trinity*.[33] Study the doctrine of God, to know it better for yourselves, and to improve your ability to teach it to others.

3. *We should labor to know the Father in a Christ-centered, Spirit-illumined manner.* Follow the structure of Paul's prayer: first he prayed for believers to be filled with the knowledge of what Christ has revealed to us, then for an understanding shaped by the Holy Spirit. Finally he prayed that believers would increase in the knowledge of the Father. If we would know the Father rightly, we must know him as declared by the Son and taught by the Spirit.

Let us never seek to know God in an abstract or purely intellectual way, in isolation from our moral and spiritual lives. Nicholas Byfield (1579-1622) gave the following rules for increasing in knowledge. First, he said, put what you already know into practice. In doing God's will, we learn more about him (John 7:17). Second, do not be drawn aside into curiosities and speculations. Cling to the Scriptures. Third, use the time well whenever you have an opportunity to learn and grow (Eph. 5:16). Do not be lazy, indifferent, fearful, or so distracted that you miss or lose the benefit of an occasion to increase in knowledge. Fourth, hold the things of the world, that pertain to this life, with a light grip. Do not let the cares of this world choke the Word and destroy faith. Fifth, confess your ignorance and need of light, and give glory to God for what you do know, and the light that you have. To fail to give God glory is to despise the knowledge you have, and to provoke him to give you over to a darkened mind (Rom. 1:21-28). Sixth, use all of God's ordinances constantly and cheerfully. The means of grace are God's appointed channels of blessing.[34]

This has huge implications for how we handle the doctrine of God, but I think the essence is this: when you aim to know God or help others to know God, keep going back to the cross. Jeremiah told us to boast only in the knowledge of God (Jer. 9:23-24). Paul said he boasted only in the cross of Christ (Gal. 6:14). Now put those together. Boast only in knowing God; boast only in Christ crucified. Only in Christ crucified can we see God's glory in a way that opens the heart to boast in him. Never separate the doctrine of God from his greatest self-revelation: Jesus Christ, the image of God. If you do, you will not promote spiritual growth. Only in Christ crucified do we find God as reconciled Father.

Conclusion

Let us seek the Spirit's grace to grow in spiritual knowledge and to help other believers to grow. The triune God has promised to give himself to his covenant people. He has bound himself in union to believers so that we might know him personally, intimately and eternally. Do not be content to wade in the shallow end of the pool! Launch out into the ocean depths of his glorious being and heavenly majesty. Go deeper. Know God. Strive to know him better tomorrow than you do today.

Remember that growth is normal for those who are spiritually alive. Proverbs 4:18 says, 'The path of the just is as the shining light, that shineth more and more unto the perfect day.' As the sun rises through the morning sky until it reaches its noon-day brightness, so should the Christian's light increase as he travels onward to the Father's house.

Furthermore, growth is necessary. Oliver Cromwell (1599-1658) wrote in his Bible: 'He who ceases to be better, ceases to be good.'[35] It is the nature of living things to grow, and if they cease growing, they are beginning to die. Christ said to a backslidden church in Revelation 3:2: 'Be watchful, and strengthen the things which remain, that are ready to die.'

Yearn to grow, pray for growth, and labor to increase more and more in the knowledge of our Lord and his will. If you find yourself indifferent, lethargic, or resistant to growing in knowledge, confess your sin and rebellion, and cry out for the grace of Christ to press on in the upward calling of God.

Today many Christians view faith as a doorway. Once you're in, you're done. But as John Bunyan reminded us, faith is a pilgrimage to a far country. It is a marathon that requires us to press forward on the course until we reach the finish line. What would we think of a runner who sat down halfway through the race and said, 'Why try to go further? Look how far I've come!' No, do not sit down, no matter how far you have come in your understanding of the Lord. Press on to know the Lord more and more each day!

2
Spiritual growth in practice

We … do not cease to pray for you … that ye might walk
worthy of the Lord unto all pleasing,
being fruitful in every good work,
and increasing in the knowledge of God
(Colossians 1:9-10).

Caleb, son of Jephunneh of the tribe of Judah, stands tall among the heroes of the faith. When God declared to Moses that the unbelieving, murmuring Israelites were to be excluded from the land of promise and condemned to wander in the wilderness until all were dead, he exempted Caleb and Joshua. Few have attained such recognition as what God said of Caleb in Numbers 14:24: 'But my servant Caleb, because he had another spirit with him, and hath followed me fully, him will I bring into the land whereinto he went; and his seed shall possess it.'

Five times Scripture says that Caleb 'wholly followed the LORD'.[36] As a man of faith, he followed the Lord sincerely, persistently, comprehensively and exclusively. When the twelve spies of Israel returned from Canaan, ten of them brought a most discouraging report: 'We are not able to go up against the people; for they are stronger than we ... we were in our own sight as grasshoppers' (Num. 13:31, 33). But Caleb said, 'Let us go up at once, and possess it; for we are well able to overcome it.' The negative report of the other spies provoked an outcry of despair among the people: 'Would God we had died in this wilderness!' In their unbelief, they decide to go back to Egypt. Once more Caleb and Joshua cry out in protest: 'If the LORD delight in us, then he will bring us into this land... Only rebel not ye against the LORD, neither fear ye the people of the land ... their defence is departed from them, and the LORD is with us' (Num 14:8-9).

Only the sudden appearance of the glory of the LORD in the tabernacle saved Caleb and Joshua from being stoned to death. While the rest of his generation perished because of unbelief, Caleb persevered in faith, fought the battles of the Lord, and finally took possession of his inheritance in the promised land. He was a man of vision, strength, courage and perseverance. These traits were all rooted in the faith worked in his heart by the Spirit of God.

Would you like to be a Caleb today? Do you want it said of you, 'There is a man who wholly follows the

Lord'? This is what spiritual growth is all about; it is acorns becoming mighty oaks, and weak sinners becoming strong like Caleb because another Spirit is in them. Achieving such a high degree of faith and obedience isn't easy, but it is possible because God's gracious Spirit is still at work today.

In some respects, personal growth is a painful process. We discover how foolish and sinful we are by nature, and how painful it is to change and to grow. But these are good growing pains. George Barlow said, 'There is no progress possible to the man who does not see and mourn over his defects.'[37] It is better to experience growing pains than to retreat into indifference and complacency. Rowland Hill said, 'Some people's religion reminds me of a rocking horse, which has motion without progress.'[38] Let's not be rocking horses; let us be plough horses for the Lord, pushing forward to accomplish the work before us, and war horses, pressing forward into the fight.

In the words of the *Heidelberg Catechism* (Q. 115), let us constantly endeavor and pray to God for the grace of the Holy Spirit, that we may become 'more and more conformable to the image of God, till we arrive at the perfection proposed to us in a life to come'.[39] In this present life our focus must be more and more on this kind of spiritual growth, if we hope to arrive at the goal of perfection in Christ in the life to come.

In the previous chapter, we examined spiritual growth in *knowledge* from Colossians 1:9-10. We saw our need to grow in our knowledge of the Father, by the Son, and in the Holy Spirit. Now we return to Colossians 1:10 to consider spiritual growth in *practice*: 'that ye might walk worthy of the Lord unto all pleasing, being fruitful in every good work'. We will see that spiritual growth proceeds along three lines: growing in Christ's pattern, growing in pleasing God, and growing in spiritual fruitfulness.

Growing in Christ's pattern

Colossians 1:10 says that Paul prayed for the Colossian Christians to be filled with knowledge 'that ye might walk worthy of the Lord'. The verb that is used here is an infinitive that expresses the purpose of being filled with that knowledge. Growth in spiritual knowledge aims for growth in spiritual practice. John Davenant wrote: 'Wisdom and spiritual understanding are poured into the minds of men from God, not for barren knowledge and idle speculation, but for the practice and exercise of holiness.'[40]

The believer's daily and comprehensive calling

This practice and exercise is to be our daily pattern of conduct. It is a pattern that is 'worthy'. This adverb[41] can mean deserving of something (Rom. 1:32; 1 Tim. 1:15), but that usage here would contradict the gospel of grace. Nothing in the text suggests merit; rather, it is full of thanksgiving that God has already given believers the title deed to heaven (Col. 1:5, 12). 'Worthy' can also mean fitting or suitable, as in 'fruits meet for [literally, 'worthy of'] repentance' (Matt. 3:8).[42] So in Colossians 1, 'worthy' means a lifestyle fitting or appropriate to the Lord; that is, one that is shaped by his teachings and commands. To 'walk worthy' of the Lord means to conduct oneself in a manner that honors our Lord Jesus Christ as he is revealed in the gospel. By implication, Paul is urging us not to live in a way that contradicts the gospel, but to live in a way that is suitable to it, as being worthy of the gospel of Christ.

This flows out of Paul's prayer in verse 9, for if God fills us with the knowledge of his saving will in Christ, the result will be that we strive to live in a way that conforms to the gospel and displays its beauty to all who are around us.

'Walking worthy of the Lord' sums up the entire calling of the Christian, as Paul writes in 1 Thessalonians 2:12, urging believers to 'walk worthy of God, who hath called you unto his kingdom and glory'. Walking worthy of the Lord, we shall be led in the path of God's kingdom to the promised glory of heaven. Such a walk summons us to live in a way that fits the pattern given to us by our Lord Jesus. It displays his glory and gives him honor. John Eadie said, 'To walk worthy of the Lord, is to feel the solemn bond of redeeming blood, to enshrine the image of Him who shed it, to breathe His spirit and act in harmony with His example.'[43]

Paul writes in Ephesians 4:1: 'I therefore, the prisoner of the Lord, beseech you that ye walk worthy of the vocation wherewith ye are called.' This is Paul's introduction to the practical section of his epistle in chapters 4 - 6, which encompasses the entire Christian life. But note what Paul says next in Ephesians 4:2-3: 'With all lowliness and meekness, with longsuffering, forbearing one another in love; endeavoring to keep the unity of the Spirit in the bond of peace'. At the top of Paul's list of the qualities of a worthy walk are humility, gentleness, endurance, patience, love for our brethren, unity in the Spirit, and the pursuit of peace.

Philippians 1:27a says, 'Let your conversation be as it becometh the gospel of Christ.' How? By standing fast 'in one spirit, with one mind striving together for the faith of the gospel; and in nothing terrified by your adversaries' (vv. 27b, 28). In chapter 2, Paul continues this appeal, citing the example of Christ in his humiliation: 'Let nothing be done through strife or vainglory; but in lowliness of mind let each esteem other better than themselves. Look not every man on his own things, but every man also on the things of others. Let this mind be in you, which was also in Christ Jesus' (2:3-5). What did Christ do? He humbled himself, took the form of a servant, and became obedient unto death (2:7-8).

The believer's call to Christlike denial and humble service

Self-humiliation and self-denial are essential for spiritual growth in practice. There is no other way to grow in Christ's pattern. Thomas Watson (*c.* 1620-1686) said, 'The right manner of growth is to grow less in one's own eyes.'[44] If it was fitting for God's sinless Son to humble himself, how much more for sinful people such as we are, to think less of ourselves as we grow in self-knowledge? This is what it means to grow down into Christ's pattern, for Christ taught us that the pattern of his kingdom was to pursue greatness by becoming a humble servant to others (Mark 10:43-45). We grow down into greatness.

What does that say, then, about professing Christians who are arrogant, bossy, harsh, insensitive, unwilling to listen, self-seeking and power-hungry? Even unbelievers can see the hypocrisy in such prideful egotism. But how beautiful is the meekness of children of God, who humble themselves to serve others and willingly take up the cross of suffering. We cannot serve Christ in any other way, for no other way is worthy of him.

When we strive to follow Christ in self-denial and humble service, we come face to face with our remaining sin. We discover that we must do more than conquer the sins of the flesh, such as drunkenness, lust, or laziness. We discover that the sins of the spirit are even more heinous in God's sight: unbelief, pride, ambition, covetousness, envy, hatred, bitterness and hardness of heart. It can be a shock to discover how much ground has to be cleared before we can begin to grow. J. I. Packer says in his book *Rediscovering Holiness:*

> Pride blows us up like balloons, but grace punctures our conceit and lets the hot, proud air out of our system. The result (a very salutary result) is that we shrink, and end up seeing ourselves as less — less nice, less able, less wise, less good, less strong, less steady, less committed... — than we thought we were. We stop kidding ourselves that we are persons of great importance to the world and to God. We settle for being insignificant and dispensable.

> Off-loading our fantasies of omnicompetence, we start trying to be trustful, obedient, dependent, patient, and willing in our relationship with God... We bow to events that rub our noses in the reality of our own weaknesses, and we look to God for strength quietly to cope.[45]

The *Heidelberg Catechism* calls this process 'the mortification' ('putting to death') of the old man, involving 'a sincere sorrow of heart that we have provoked God by our sins, and more and more to hate them and flee from them'. In other words, the old self must be pulled down from its throne, and sin must be assailed and subdued, for Christ's sake.

We then experience that spiritual growth entails what John the Baptist professed in John 3:30: 'He [Christ] must increase, but I must decrease.' We also experience the answer to the prayer of the *Heidelberg Catechism* (Q. 123): 'Rule us so by Thy Word and Spirit, that we may submit ourselves more and more to Thee.'[46] We grow in humility to live a life worthy of Christ.

Useful applications

Here are two implications of growing in Christ's pattern:

1. *Mature Christians act like servants, not lords.* Matthew 20:25–27 says, 'But Jesus called them unto him, and said, Ye know that the princes of the Gentiles exercise dominion over them, and they that are great exercise authority upon them. But it shall not be so among you: but whosoever will be great among you, let him be your minister; and whosoever will be chief among you, let him be your servant.'

There is nothing wrong with exercising authority. Scripture often teaches that God has appointed people in authority in various social spheres and expects us to obey them.[47] The issue is how they exercise that authority. Paul, who was an apostle and thus was one of the highest officers of the church, said in 2 Corinthians 4:5: 'For we preach not ourselves, but Christ Jesus the Lord; and ourselves your servants for Jesus' sake.'

It is somewhat ironic today to hear the words of Matthew 20:26:'Whosoever will be great among you, let him be your minister.' Too many ministers take those words literally! I grieve that the pastoral office is sometimes abused by men who seek honor and power for themselves — and pray that I'm not one of them. But of course 'minister' here means 'servant'.[48] Ministers of the church should thus be the most humble, gentle, forbearing men in the entire congregation. When such men have disagreements, each should be first to show patience and seek peace. Each should defer to the other in honor, and reject worldly hierarchies. In a word, each should be like Christ.

2. *Spiritual growth encourages submission to God.* When Christ is called a servant, that does not only mean that he served other people, but it first and foremost means that he obeyed his Father. 'He humbled himself, and became obedient unto death, even the death of the cross,' says Philippians 2:8. Isaiah 42:1 thus calls Christ, 'my servant, whom I uphold; mine elect, in whom my soul delighteth'.

We tend to think of spiritual growth in terms of doing great things (and winning lots of accolades). But a large part of spiritual growth is deepening submission whereby we say, even in the shadow of the cross, 'Not my will but thine be done.' Luther once quipped that letting God be God is half of all true religion. Submission to difficult commands is the core of Christlikeness (John 10:17-18). If a commandment of God is exceedingly hard for you to obey right now, this is the point where God desires to stretch and grow you.

We must also grow in submission to difficult providences. It is a profound mystery that Christ's sufferings overflow into his people.[49] This is especially the case for Christ's ministers, as Paul explains in 2 Corinthians. Our very sufferings are part of God's method for building his kingdom. Let us learn then to be quiet under the rod. Let us learn to bear meekly the unjust afflictions that come to us through men. Let them purpose evil against us; for they are but God's hammer and chisel to sculpt us into the image of Christ.

Brothers, do we think we can follow Christ without taking up our cross and denying ourselves? If we are to experience true spiritual growth, we must grow down into Christ's pattern of humility. And let us not become discouraged. The distance between our conduct and Christ's is immense. But Christ himself is with us. Calvin said, 'Let us not cease to do the utmost, that we may incessantly go forward in the way of the Lord; and let us not despair because of the smallness of our accomplishment.'[50]

Growing in pleasing God

Colossians 1:10 says Paul prayed 'that ye might walk worthy of the Lord *unto all pleasing*'. As sinners our aim in life was to please ourselves. As Christians, our aim must be to please Christ. 'All pleasing' means that we should aim to please him in *every* way, and likewise, that we should cease from anything that displeases him, or detracts from his pleasure in us. First Thessalonians 4:1 says, 'Furthermore then we beseech you, brethren, and exhort you by the Lord Jesus, that as ye have received of us how ye ought to walk and to please God, so you would abound more and more.'

The believer's growth inseparable from serving God's pleasure

Ministers are called to serve God's pleasure, not man's.[51] Paul thus says in 1 Thessalonians 2:4: 'But as we were allowed of God to be put in trust with the gospel, even so we speak; not as pleasing men, but God, which trieth our hearts.' In Ephesians 6:6, Paul speaks contemptuously of servants who render mere 'eyeservice, as menpleasers'. John records that 'among the chief rulers also many believed in him [Christ]; but because of the Pharisees they did not confess him ... for they loved the praise of men more than the praise of God' (John 12:42-43). Since we are constantly tempted as public speakers and church leaders to court the favor of men, we must constantly remind ourselves that we called to serve an audience of One.

Calvin said this 'is such a life as, leaving the opinions of men, and leaving, in short, all carnal inclination, is regulated so as to be in subjection to God alone'.[52] That means learning what God's will is from the Bible, and doing it. Nicholas Byfield wrote: 'Thou must let the will of God, revealed in his word, be the rule of all thy actions, "a light to thy feet, and a lantern to thy paths" [Ps. 119:105, *cf*. Geneva Bible, 1560]; for in the word is contained both what he requires and what will please him.'[53]

Striving to please the Lord must continue until the final judgement. Paul writes in 2 Corinthians 5:9-10: 'Wherefore we labor, that, whether present or absent, we may be accepted of him. For we must all appear before the judgement seat of Christ; that every one may receive the things done in his body, according to that he hath done, whether it be good or bad.' Knowing that we must give such an account of our labors in the ministry, and for our care of the souls of our people (Heb. 13:17) we should do all in our power to please the Lord, to be acceptable in his sight.

The believer's relationship to justification and sanctification

In these passages the apostle Paul takes nothing away from our right standing with God as sinners justified by faith in Jesus Christ. Nonetheless, ministers are stewards of Christ, tending to his sheep, acting in his name, under his direction. 'Moreover it is required in stewards, that a man be found faithful' (1 Cor. 4:1–2). The ministry is a high calling, entailing an equally high degree of accountability to Christ. Each minister's work shall be tried by fire: 'If any man's work shall be burned he shall suffer loss: but he himself shall be saved; yet so as by fire' (1 Cor. 3:15).

Some might stumble over the word *all* in Paul's term *all pleasing*, arguing that, surely, this refers to our justification. God is totally pleased with us because of Christ's righteousness imputed to us. That is our only hope on Judgement Day. Anything else would be legalism and a denial of justification by faith alone. In response to this concern, I would say that Paul certainly had justification in mind when writing 2 Corinthians 5. After all, he concluded the chapter by saying, 'For he hath made him to be sin for us, who knew no sin; that we might be made the righteousness of God in him.' The great exchange of imputation is that our sins are put on Christ and Christ's righteousness is put on us. God accepts us as pleasing to him only because of Christ.

But in 2 Corinthians 5:9–10 Paul says, 'we labor'. He also says, 'Every one may receive the things done in his body, according to that he hath done.' So he is plainly talking here about pleasing God with our works. This is in accord with Colossians 1:10, in which Paul says, 'That ye might walk worthy of the Lord unto all pleasing, being fruitful in every good work.'

The imputation of Christ's righteousness to believers does not abolish their duty to do good works. Justification is unto sanctification. Moreover, the good works we do are evidence that God has indeed begun a good work in us. The *Belgic Confession* (art. 24) says that the 'works which God has commanded in His Word … as they proceed from the good root of faith, are good and acceptable in the sight of God, forasmuch as they are all sanctified by his grace; howbeit they are of no account towards our justification… In the meantime we do not deny that God rewards our good works, but it is through grace that He crowns His gifts.'[54] 'The righteous LORD loveth righteousness; his countenance doth behold the upright' (Ps. 11:7).

So it was that Davenant could write: 'The person of a godly and faithful man is always pleasing and acceptable to God, because he is regarded by God not as he is in himself, but as a member under Christ the head. "But there is no condemnation to them who are in Christ Jesus" (Rom. 8:1).'[55] What does this imply for our good works? Not that we are free of any duty to do good works, but that however imperfect they may be, they are pleasing to God. 'The good works of the faithful, although imperfect, are nevertheless pleasing to God, because they are regarded by him as by a loving Father, not as an austere judge.'[56] We see again how important the doctrine of adoption is in every aspect of our spiritual growth. We can please God only because he is our reconciled Father for Christ's sake.

Useful applications

Spiritual growth thus means growing as a humble believer whose works are increasingly pleasing to the Lord in every way for Christ's sake. What implications does this have for our lives?

1. *We must reorient our lives so that we increasingly seek to please God rather than men.* We must reckon with what the Bible calls the 'frowardness of the wicked' (Prov. 2:14). The fallen heart is turned away ('fro') from God. The *Heidelberg Catechism* describes the problem in the plainest terms: 'I am prone by nature to hate God and my neighbor' (Q. 5). To follow Christ, the naturally fallen heart and will must be reoriented. Paul records how the Thessalonians 'turned to God from idols to serve the living and true God; and to wait for his Son from heaven' (1 Thess. 1:9-10). This act of turning to God is called 'conversion'. But as the *Heidelberg Catechism* also teaches, the process of reorienting our hearts and lives goes on from that point to the end of our lives on earth. We embrace God's law as a rule for our lives, 'that all our life time we may learn more and more to know our sinful nature, and thus become the more earnest in seeking the remission of sin and righteousness in Christ; likewise, that we may become more and more conformable to the image of God, till we arrive at the perfection proposed to us in a life to come' (Q. 115).

The fear of the Lord should also motivate us to seek greater consistency between the faith we proclaim and the lives we lead. It is too easy for pastors to become professional in their piety. The pose of godliness adopted for the pulpit is cast off in the parking lot. Is our religion only a show or performance for the benefit of the churchgoing public? God forbid. We must live to please the Lord.

We must discipline ourselves to see the whole of our life and work in the light of Judgement Day. This will have a cleansing, clarifying effect on our motivations. We will rid ourselves of distractions, and devote ourselves to pleasing the One who is our only Lord and Master. A proper fear of God will not hinder spiritual growth but rather, encourage it. Proverbs 14:27 says, 'The fear of the LORD is a fountain of life, to depart from the snares of death.'

2. *We must expect our gracious reward from God.* We can twist the doctrine of total depravity into an excuse for doing nothing, since anything we did would be stained with sin. But this is not the case for regenerated and justified people. The children of God *do* please their Father with their obedience. Why would Paul pray that the Colossians might walk 'unto all pleasing', if there was no possibility of them doing so? Did Paul err from the truth when he told the Philippians that their financial gift was 'well pleasing to God' (Phil. 4:18)? Although 'the holiest men, while in this life, have only a small beginning of this obedience; yet so, that with a sincere resolution they begin to live, not only according to some, but all the commandments of God' (*Heidelberg Cat.*, Q. 114). So John can say, 'We keep his commandments, and do those things that are pleasing in

his sight' (1 John 3:22). This is one of the grandest results of Christ's cross (Heb. 13:20–21).

It is biblical for us to believe that God is pleased with our obedience, despite its faults, and he will one day graciously reward us for it. Christ warns us not to be hypocrites whose aim is to impress men by performing their religious duties in a public, self-aggrandizing way. Rather, we are to give and pray and fast in secret. He says, 'Thy Father which seeth in secret himself shall reward thee openly' (Matt. 6:4, 6, 18). Yes, we must grieve over our many failings and glacially slow progress in sanctification. But if we walk with integrity in our calling and in our homes, we may live in holy anticipation of hearing the Lord say, 'Well done, thou good and faithful servant: thou hast been faithful over a few things, I will make thee ruler over many things: enter thou into the joy of thy lord' (Matt. 25:21, 23). Jesus went so far as to promise in Matthew 10:42 that 'whosoever shall give to drink unto one of these little ones a cup of cold water only in the name of a disciple, verily I say unto you, he shall in no wise lose his reward'. Such a hope should spur us on to do much good and to grow.

Growing in spiritual fruitfulness

Colossians 1:10 expands the idea of walking in a way worthy of the Lord and pleasing to him to include 'being fruitful in every good work'. Earlier, in verse 6, Paul wrote about how the gospel 'bringeth forth fruit', using the same verb.[57] Having prayed that believers would be filled with the knowledge of the gospel, Paul anticipates that this knowledge will produce good fruit in them. The gospel of grace produces the fruit of good works, for it unites men to Christ, as branches are joined to a vine. Thus Paul prays in Philippians 1:11 that believers will be 'filled with the fruits of righteousness, which are by Jesus Christ, unto the glory and praise of God'.

Notice that just as Paul writes of being 'filled' in Colossians 1:9 and walking 'unto *all* pleasing' in verse 10, so also in verse 10 he speaks of producing '*every* good work'. He is praying for an abundant harvest in the lives of Christian believers. Think of an apple tree loaded with large, ripe, luscious apples. Christians should pray and labor to be like that in their good works towards others. First Corinthians 15:58 says, 'Therefore, my beloved brethren, be ye steadfast, unmovable, always abounding in the work of the Lord, forasmuch as ye know that your labor is not in vain in the Lord.'

The believer's call to a healthy activism

The fruit of grace is good works, not merely good attitudes. Scripture promotes a healthy kind of activism, which emphasizes doing, just as verse 9 emphasizes knowledge. 'Be ye doers of the word, and not hearers only' (James 1:22).

Note also that this fruit is not the people we may bring to Christ by our preaching or personal evangelism. It is entirely up to God how he uses our ministry of the Word in the lives of others. If winning over large numbers of people is the standard of ministerial fruitfulness and success, then all the prophets from Moses to Christ were dismal failures. We must concentrate on obeying God and leave the results to him.

The believer's call to abide in Christ

How do we become increasingly fruitful Christians? We immediately think of our Lord's parable of the vine: 'I am the vine, ye are the branches: he that abideth in me, and I in him, the same bringeth forth much fruit: for without me ye can do nothing' (John 15:5). We abide in Christ by faith, drawing life from him like a branch draws sap up from its roots. This is why Paul prays for spiritual knowledge prior to practical obedience. But we continue in faith, and grow in fruitfulness, according to Christ, by abiding in him. He says in John 15:7: 'If ye abide in me, and my words abide in you, ye shall ask what ye will, and it shall be done unto you.' The word of Christ, dwelling in us richly, will produce the fruits that God loves to see.

Let us now look at how we can use the Word and all other means of grace as God's tools to grow his people. The spiritual disciplines require diligent use, if we are to profit from them. They must become part of the fabric of our lives, as spiritual disciplines that we follow, in private, as families, among our fellow believers, and in the community at large.[58]

The believer's growth through spiritual disciplines

I will touch on sixteen disciplines in all, four in each category. In reality, all these disciplines are different ways to exercise ourselves and others through two primary means: the Word and prayer, or listening to God and speaking to God.[59] The Word and prayer then combine into one great means: the exercise of faith in Christ. But there are different ways to make use of the Word and prayer. If we are conscious of our weakness, we will not complain about the number of supports God gives us. Let us consider some of the supports God gives us and others to grow spiritually.

Think of the list of sixteen disciplines as a catalog of books you receive from a great book publisher. You can't buy everything in the catalog (sadly!), but you can buy two or three books. So you flip through the catalog and circle the books that most appeal to you. That is what I want you to do as we work our way through the catalog of spiritual disciplines. In your mind (or in your notes), circle the ones that you need to work on most, then invest yourself in getting a grip on them.

Growing through private disciplines

Private time devoted to communion with God is central to growth. Austin Phelps (1820-1890) said, 'We may lay it down as an elementary principle of religion that no large growth in holiness was ever gained by one who did not take time to be often, and long alone with God.'[60] Consider these four major disciplines of personal devotion.

1. Read the Scriptures

Our Lord says in John 17:17: 'Sanctify them through thy truth: thy word is truth.' Psalm 119:11 says, 'Thy word have I hid in mine heart, that I might not sin against thee.' So read the Bible daily. Follow a plan to read through the entire Bible in a reasonable cycle of time. If you are one of Christ's sheep, constantly expose your mind to the voice of your Shepherd. The Bible echoes with the voice of he who laid down his life for you.

The *Westminster Larger Catechism* (Q. 157) offers good advice on how to read the Bible for spiritual growth. The Holy Scriptures are to be read:

- With a high and reverent esteem of them (Ps. 19:10; Neh. 8:3-10; Exod. 24:7; 2 Chron. 34:27; Isa. 66:2).
- With the firm persuasion that they are the very words of God (2 Peter 1:19-21), and only he can enable us to understand them (Luke 24:45; 2 Cor. 3:13-16).

- With a desire to know, believe and obey the will of God revealed in them (Deut. 17:19-20).
- With diligence (Acts 17:11) and attention to the matter and scope of them (Acts 8:30-34; Luke 10:26-28).
- With meditation (Ps. 1:2; 119:97), application (2 Chron. 34:21), self-denial (Prov. 3:5; Deut. 33:3), and prayer (Prov. 2:1-6; Ps. 119:18; Neh. 8:6-8).[61]

Don't neglect to sing the Scriptures, either, in your private devotion. Use the metrical versions of the Psalms in *The Psalter* to feed your soul and glorify God. If you can't carry a tune, get CDs or digital files of music. In singing praise to God, you will find him to be your refuge. Psalm 59:16-17 says, 'But I will sing of thy power; yea, I will sing aloud of thy mercy in the morning: for thou hast been my defense and refuge in the day of my trouble. Unto thee, O my strength, will I sing: for God is my defense, and the God of my mercy.'

2. Meditate on the Bible

Psalm 1 describes the blessed man this way: 'his delight is in the law of the LORD; and in his law doth he meditate day and night' (Ps. 1:2). Colossians 3:1-2 says, 'If ye then be risen with Christ, seek those things which are above, where Christ sitteth on the right hand of God. Set your affection [literally, set your minds] on things above, not on things on the earth.'

The Puritans often spoke of meditating on God's Word. Meditation is the intentional setting of the mind upon various truths to press them deeply into the heart. Here are some suggestions from the Puritans on how to meditate. First, pray for the power to focus your mind on the Word. Second, read the Bible and select a verse or two. Third, repeat those verses to yourself in order to memorize them, saying them ten times while looking at the page, then ten times while looking away. Repeat them once a day for retention.

Fourth, think about what these verses say and imply, probing the book of Scripture (other verses on the same topic), the book of conscience (how you have believed or disbelieved, obeyed or disobeyed), and the book of nature (how this truth appears in experience and the world). Fifth, stir your affections unto love, desire, grief, hope, zeal and joy, as appropriate. Preach the text to yourself with powerful application. Sixth, arouse your soul to the specific duty that the text requires, making holy resolutions for the glory of God. Seventh, conclude with prayers for divine assistance, thanksgiving for graces given, and singing psalms of praise to God.

At first this may seem complicated, rather like learning how to ride a bicycle. But once you get it down, meditation will become part of who you are. As Christ's word dwells within you, Christ himself will dwell within you in increasing measure.

3. Pray and work

Nehemiah is a great example of praying and working every day, sometimes simultaneously. This dependent activism allowed Nehemiah to say in Nehemiah 2:20: 'The God of heaven, he will prosper us; therefore we his servants will arise and build.' When the enemies of the Jews conspired against them, Nehemiah took the danger in his stride, saying, 'We made our prayer unto our God, and set a watch against them day and night' (Neh. 4:9). And so it went, day by day, praying, watching, and building, in the faith that God would prosper his people, and deliver them from the hand of their enemies.

Prayer and work are like two oars in a rowboat: using just one oar moves you in circles. To reach the other shore, you need to use both oars at once. God intended prayer and work to go together. Constant petition and careful planning are friends, not enemies. Begin each day by looking at the tasks that lie ahead of you. Go to the Lord saying, 'Lord, I cannot do this myself. Please give me Thy divine help.' Then proceed to labor in your calling trusting in and counting on the God who answers prayer. After finishing the task, confess your sins and failures, and thank God, giving him the glory for every drop of ability, for the wisdom obtained, and for everything accomplished, and every trial sustained.

Above all earthly needs, pray for the Spirit. Archibald

Alexander (1772-1851) wrote: 'Pray constantly and fervently for the influences of the Holy Spirit. No blessing is so particularly and emphatically promised in answer to prayer as this.'[62]

To sustain the discipline of prayer, give yourself to it. Give prayer priority over other tasks. Give prayer your heart, not just your outward performance. Devote set times in your day to pray. Mingle prayer with meditation on the Word, so that you are praying back to God his own words. Pray by faith in the whole Trinity: the Father as the Hearer of your prayers, the Son as the Holiness of your prayers, and the Spirit as the Helper of your prayers. Find a place of solitude to pray. The Puritans designated a certain place in their homes such as a large closet or small room as the prayer room. Commit yourself to pray every time you feel an impulse to pray. Learn to pray with your eyes open.

4. Keep a journal

The book of Psalms and the book of Nehemiah attest to the value of writing out devotions. While journaling is not commanded in Scripture, it is a helpful means of obeying God's commands to remember his works and to pass them on to future generations.[63] Writing can also help you to pour out your heart to the Lord, for sometimes thoughts come through our fingers that would never make it out of our mouths. It helps to write them down because you can see your own thoughts before you. Some might view journaling as a product of a bygone era, but I have grown a great deal by writing things down. One of our elders writes a blog once or twice a week and he has grown and flourished from it. Find a way to creatively express your meditations and prayers.

Growing through family disciplines

North America is a very individualistic culture, and this affects our spirituality. But in the Bible spiritual growth is very much a matter of relationships, beginning with the family. Of course, the most powerful influence we can have in our families is our personal example of godliness. There is no substitute for walking what you talk. But there are also domestic means of grace that greatly assist the family in spiritual growth. Let me suggest four disciplines of family life that will promote a fruitful Christian life.

1. Release the power of regular family worship and catechizing

Ephesians 6:4 says the head of the household has the responsibility to teach Christianity to his children: 'And, ye fathers, provoke not your children to wrath: but bring them up in the nurture and admonition of the Lord.' The Lord has a multi-generational vision for his people. Psalm 78:5-6 says, 'For he established a testimony in Jacob, and appointed a law in Israel, which he commanded our fathers, that they should make them known to their children: that the generation to come might know them, even the children which should be born; who should arise and declare them to their children.'

I would guess that the typical American family spends its evenings in one of two ways. Either they rush around to meetings, sports events, social activities, or they sit down and spend a few hours staring at the television or a computer screen. The idea of gathering as a family every evening to read the Bible, talk about the things of the Lord, sing his praises, and pray, probably seems impossible or unattainable to most people. Who has time for family worship? Yet this discipline is desperately needed today, and it is very possible if we say no to other things.

Family worship should not be a burden but a delight. Arrange your schedules so that you can have a brief devotion in the morning, then a longer time (perhaps twenty or thirty minutes) in the evening. Connect it to eating together so that it becomes a part of your daily rhythm. Have a plan for what you do. Read some Scripture. Memorize a catechism question and answer. Pray briefly together. In the evening, lead a discussion by asking questions of your children based on a Scripture passage or catechism question. Sing the Psalms and other good songs based on sound doctrine.[64]

Do you want Christ to fill your home and your family relationships? Welcome him into your house in regular family worship.

2. Make your home the center of hospitality and fellowship for others.

God commands us in 1 Peter 4:9: 'Use hospitality one to another without grudging.' Hospitality requires planning and may cost you time, money and effort. It need not be lavish; the point of Christian hospitality is not to impress others, or to exploit them for your own ends. You might pick one night a week as your regular hospitality night, on which you invite someone over to share in your regular meal and family devotions. This is a great way to develop friendships in church, to reach out to unbelieving neighbors, to encourage your officers, to support missionaries, to care for widows and single people, and to train your children to serve others.

Hebrews 13:1-2 says, 'Let brotherly love continue. Be not forgetful to entertain strangers: for thereby some have entertained angels unawares.' Those who show hospitality to others receive unexpected blessings. This discipline seems like a great effort, but it adds up to much profit for your family — spiritually and relationally.

Hospitality is another way of welcoming Christ into your home. Remember that Christ will one day say, 'Come, ye blessed of my Father, inherit the kingdom prepared for you from the foundation of the world: for I was hungered, and ye gave me meat: I was thirsty, and ye gave me drink: I was a stranger, and ye took me in....Verily I say unto you,

Inasmuch as ye have done it unto one of the least of these my brethren, ye have done it unto me' (Matt. 25:34–35, 40). When was the last time you had someone over to your home for a meal and had meaningful fellowship?

3. Discipline your children in love

A rebuke to the ear and a rod to the bottom can both serve as a spiritual discipline. Proverbs 22:15 says, 'Foolishness is bound in the heart of a child; but the rod of correction shall drive it far from him.' God uses discipline mixed with the gospel to restrain and mortify original sin. Discipline thus expresses love. Proverbs 13:24 says, 'He that spareth his rod hateth his son: but he that loveth him chasteneth him betimes.'

Always combine the rod with the law and the gospel. Use disobedience as an opportunity to share the gospel. Teach your children to seek reconciliation with others by confession and restitution, and to seek reconciliation with God through Christ's atonement. Let the gospel guide you to discipline, not in wrath or judicial retribution, but to train your children for their good. That is what the Father does for his children. Be neither harsh nor lax. Aim not so much at perfect performance as submission of the will. Above all, set up rules, be consistent, and acknowledge your own failures with repentance.

4. Counsel your children in major decisions

Proverbs 23:22 says, 'Hearken unto thy father that begat thee, and despise not thy mother when she is old.' Parents should be guides and counselors even after children grow up. The father says to the son in Proverbs 23:26: 'My son, give me thine heart, and let thine eyes observe my ways.' Nurture a relationship of trust, respect and imitation with your children.

As your children grow towards adulthood, your influence over them will include less coercive power and more moral authority. You cannot be your child's 'buddy', but you should aim to become his older friend and counselor. Once he graduates from your home, your influence will be minimal.

Your influence will be especially significant in helping your child make decisions that affect the rest of their lives. You know your child better than anyone else, so help him to choose a vocation that is well suited to his gifts and temperament. Assist your children in finding mates who are godly and loving; prepared to fulfill their biblical roles as husband and wife; mature in conduct and motivation; a good match in social, intellectual, and financial backgrounds; and attractive to each other. Young adults are not looking for parents who are dictators, but they greatly appreciate leaning on you as a trusted friend whose wisdom can guide them in vexing situations.

These then are the disciplines of family worship, hospitality, discipline, and counsel. When you practice them, you, as the head of the household, will open your home to Christ and his sacred influences so that your wife will be like a fruitful vine and your children like saplings around your table.

Growing through corporate disciplines

By corporate disciplines, I mean those relating to our lives as part of the body of Christ. When Paul says we are members of Christ's body, he teaches us that we are vitally connected with Christ and with other Christians, in the fellowship of the church. Christ meets us through the body. Ephesians 4:15-16 says, 'But speaking the truth in love, [we] may grow up into him in all things, which is the head, even Christ: from whom the whole body fitly joined together and compacted by that which every joint supplieth, according to the effectual working in the measure of every part, maketh increase of the body unto the edifying of itself in love.' Let us consider four key disciplines for growth through the church.

1. The hearing of the preached Word

Preaching is the Holy Spirit's chosen means to create and nurture faith in Christ. Romans 10:17 says, 'So then faith cometh by hearing, and hearing by the word of God.' Therefore train yourself and those under your authority to treat sermons like food. Christ says in Luke 8:18, 'Take heed therefore how ye hear.' Be good soil to receive God's seed. Preachers, beware of always being the speaker and never the listener. Listen to good sermons regularly.

Here are some instructions for good listening. Prepare to hear the Word by praying for your soul and for the preacher. Come with an appetite for truth and a humble, teachable heart. Work hard to pay attention and push away wandering thoughts. Receive the Word with meekness, not as a judge or critic, but as a sinner before the throne of grace. Talk about the sermon afterwards to remember it and apply it. Put the Word into practice. Do not just be a hearer but a doer of the Word, lest you build your house on sand instead of the rock foundation of Christ. If something from the sermon blesses you, share this blessing with others.

For those of us who are preachers, we need to put substantial, God-glorifying, Christ-centered, soul-edifying food for believers to feast upon, and for the Spirit to use in working faith in the hearts of unbelievers. We must ask ourselves if our sermons are suitable as nourishment for our hearers. Do we serve a substantial meal, or just crumbs? Are we giving our people stones for bread? Are we feeding strong meat to mere babes in Christ? Are we forcing mature believers to subsist on a diet of milk alone. It is all very well to teach people to listen conscientiously, but why should they bother if there is little real help or value offered to them in our preaching?

2. Make diligent use of the sacraments

We may not separate the sacraments from the Word any more than we may separate the Word from the Spirit. In the light of the Word, the sacraments are signs that point us to Christ, and to the central moments of his work as the Mediator, his holy conception and birth; his redemptive suffering; his trials, crucifixion and death; his resurrection and ascension into heaven; and his coming again to judge the world. Our Lord commands us: 'This do in remembrance of me' (1 Cor. 11:24). Just as the sacraments commemorate the work of Christ, they also are a means of fellowship with the person of Christ. First Corinthians 10:16 says, 'The cup of blessing which we bless, is it not the communion of the blood of Christ? The bread which we break, is it not the communion of the body of Christ?' Christ calls us to his table in order to feed and nourish our hungry and thirsty souls with his crucified body and blood, 'the true meat and drink of life eternal'.[65] Eating the bread, drinking from the cup, we lift up our hearts to Christ in heaven on high, expecting through the Holy Spirit's working to be fed and refreshed in our souls, with his body and blood.[66]

Let me speak a word specifically to ministers on this point. We face a real danger of becoming professional and hypocritical in the use of corporate means of grace. It is all too easy to lapse into rut of custom or the trap of superstition. The sacraments cease to be means of grace, and become mere empty rituals. Both for those who administer the sacraments, and those who receive them, Scripture commands us to prepare beforehand, by examining ourselves as to our repentance from sin, our faith in Christ, and the reality of our Christian discipleship; and by considering the end for which the sacraments were instituted. Every Christian should know how to 'improve' his baptism,[67] and what is required of communicants, before, during and after the time of administration.[68]

It is possible for ministers to be caught up in the mere logistics of administration, and lose sight of the great end for which Christ instituted baptism and the Holy Supper. To help you to seek Christ in the Supper, let me recommend reading Wilhelmus à Brakel's treatment of 'The Practice of the Lord's Supper Consisting in Preparation, Celebration, and Reflection' in *The Christian's Reasonable Service*.[69] It is rich.

3. Participate in fellowship in the church

Acts 2:42 describes the Spirit-filled church: 'And they continued steadfastly in the apostles' doctrine and fellowship, and in breaking of bread, and in prayers.' Proverbs 13:20 says, 'He that walketh with wise men shall be wise: but a companion of fools shall be destroyed.' Build friendships with godly men and women who can be an example, encouragement, comfort and correction to you. Association begets assimilation, Thomas Watson said. The person who isolates himself defies sound wisdom (Prov. 18:1). Don't wait around for someone to invite you over. Make use of the opportunities for fellowship in the church, and invite others to come with you.

4. Sanctify the Lord's Day

Isaiah 58:13-14 says, 'If thou turn away thy foot from the sabbath, from doing thy pleasure on my holy day; and call the sabbath a delight, the holy of the LORD, honourable; and shalt honour him, not doing thine own ways, nor finding thine own pleasure, nor speaking thine own words: then shalt thou delight thyself in the LORD; and I will cause thee to ride upon the high places of the earth, and feed thee with the heritage of Jacob thy father: for the mouth of the LORD hath spoken it.'

Make the entire Sabbath a time of worship and spiritual delight. Just as a man sets aside other concerns to take his wife out so that he can focus on her and their relationship, consider the Lord's Day, reverently speaking, as a 'sacred date' with God to grow and celebrate your relationship with him. Give yourself time to meditate, pray, praise, fellowship, and study for personal enrichment when you are at home. Avoid making this a day of excessive busyness in church matters.

Corporate disciplines provide access to resources for spiritual growth that we cannot have by ourselves.

Growing through neighborly disciplines

Earlier I talked about growing down into Christ's pattern of servanthood. Serving others obviously focuses on washing the feet of the saints. But it is not limited to the church. We must follow in the footsteps of our Lord to love the lost world. Kent Hughes says, 'Any doctrine which isolates the believer from the needs of the world is not a spiritual doctrine.'[70]

Matthew 9:35-38 says, 'Jesus went about all the cities and villages, teaching in their synagogues, and preaching the gospel of the kingdom, and healing every sickness and every disease among the people. But when he saw the multitudes, he was moved with compassion on them, because they fainted, and were scattered abroad, as sheep having no shepherd. Then saith he unto his disciples, The harvest truly is plenteous, but the laborers are few; pray ye therefore the Lord of the harvest, that he will send forth laborers into his harvest.'

In this text we see four patterns of Christ's servanthood that we can implement as disciplines in our own lives.

1. Evangelize sinners with the gospel

Christ had an itinerant ministry of preaching in 'all the cities and villages'. Most of us are settled in one place and one church. But we should work to spread the gospel within our sphere of influence — and beyond.

Preachers and teachers should regularly aim some of their messages at unbelievers. There are unconverted adults and children in your church; don't let them drift into the assumption that they are saved by baptism and behavior. Mix into your sermon series entire messages devoted to calling unbelievers to Christ. My colleague at seminary, Dr David Murray, speaks of four types of evangelistic sermons:

- 'warm-up' sermons that address common objections to Christianity;
- 'warning' sermons that awaken sinners by focusing on something like the nature of God, his holy law, their sin, or the judgement to come;
- 'wooing' sermons that display the wondrous love of Christ and his all-sufficient work;
- and 'whosoever will' sermons that summon sinners to repent and trust in Christ, believing that God uses his Word to give life to dead sinners.[71]

Pray for opportunities to speak the gospel in personal conversation. Stay alert for God's answers to those prayers, and snatch opportunities to speak with Spirit-filled boldness. Colossians 4:2-6 says, 'Continue in prayer, and watch in the same with thanksgiving; withal praying also for us, that God would open unto us a door of utterance, to speak the mystery of Christ, for which I am also in bonds: that I may make it manifest, as I ought to speak. Walk in wisdom toward them that are without, redeeming the time. Let your speech be always with grace, seasoned with salt, that ye may know how ye ought to answer every man.'

2. Serve people with your time and money

Our Lord went about doing good, 'healing every sickness and every disease among the people'. His miracles were signs of the kingdom of God, confirming the gospel of the kingdom with mighty demonstrations of divine compassion (Luke 7:20-23). Today we must point people to the reality of God's kingdom and the truth of the gospel with acts of love. The merciful and the peacemakers are the salt of the earth and the light of the world today.

We do not want to fall into the ditch of replacing the gospel with social action, but we also do not want to close our hearts to the poor. We must love others with word and deed. We must seek the good of others both politically and socially. This may cost us time, money and emotional stress. But it will also glorify God and help us to grow.

3. Have compassion on people but flee worldliness

Christ 'was moved with compassion on them, because they fainted, and were scattered abroad, as sheep having no shepherd'. Our hearts should break at the plight of sinners in this world. They are not safe in the fold of the shepherd but are exposed to the ravenous wolves of the devil. They need Christ or they will be lost for ever! Should we not weep for them? Were we not once among them? Oh, may God give us a heart for the lost!

But in our compassion we must remember that they are a people with no king (1 Kings 22:17). Everyone does what is right in his own eyes (Judges 21:25). Therefore we must love unbelievers but separate ourselves from their wicked ways. One of the tragedies of the contemporary church is that it thinks we must become like the world to win the world. In reality, we must love sinners but we must be different from them.

Beware of living a divided life as if you could give part of it to God and part to the world. Alexander wrote: 'Another thing which prevents growth in grace is that Christians do not make their obedience to Christ comprehend every other object of pursuit. Their religion is too much a separate thing, and they pursue their worldly business in another spirit ... Serve God in the field and in the shop, in buying and in selling and getting gain.'[72]

Spiritual growth requires that we cast off worldliness with its lust of the eyes, lust of the flesh, and pride of life. Such idolatrous love of the creature poisons the books, videos, music, recreation, entertainment, clothing styles, educational systems, art, business practices, and philosophies of the world. Some professing Christians embrace these things, and call it a ministry. But if salt loses its saltiness, its distinctive flavor is gone and it becomes worthless. In the end the church is trampled under the world's foot and despised precisely because it is like the world.

But the Christian who is growing spiritually rises up with a willingness to be persecuted for righteousness's sake because he hungers and thirsts for righteousness and longs to be pure in spirit. He says to the world, 'I love you,' then shows the world that love is something more sacred and clean than the world could imagine.

Divine love flows out of the gospel in holiness and mercy. Remember, we are talking about how being filled with divine knowledge moves us to walk in a manner worthy of the Lord. Thomas Scott (1747-1821) wrote: 'The admiring contemplation of the glory of the Lord, in the person and salvation of Christ, is always productive of a gradual transformation of the soul into his holy image.'[73]

How does this affect our love for people? Scott said, 'And the Saviour in condescending and compassionate love, to the very persons whose crimes he most deeply abhorred, appears peculiarly beautiful and endearing to the redeemed sinner. Thus benevolent love to mankind in general is produced and increased; selfish and contracted prejudices are removed.'[74] The better we know Christ, the more we will become unlike the world yet love the world.

4. Intercede for the world

Christ commanded us: 'Pray ye therefore the Lord of the harvest, that he will send forth laborers into his harvest.' How will the world believe in Christ if it has not heard his gospel? How will it hear without a preacher? And how will anyone preach unless he has been raised up, trained, and sent by the Lord of the harvest? Pray therefore that God would raise up laborers to preach all over the world. Have a map or atlas in front of you when you pray. Use *Operation World* to guide your prayers for every day. Christ's concern was not just for the cities but also for the villages. Pray for the villages around you, that God would send them laborers of love who will declare the glory of God through the only Mediator Jesus Christ. Pray for the seminaries, too, that they would be workshops of the Holy Spirit for crafting men. Get down on your knees, and lift up your eyes to see the harvest fields.

If we are going to grow into the image of Christ, we must learn to love our neighbors as ourselves. Here are four neighborly disciplines to promote spiritual growth: evangelize with the gospel, serve others with our time and money, have compassion on others without worldliness, and pray for the world.

This completes our catalog of disciplines to be 'fruitful in every good work' (Col. 1:10). As we went through the catalog, what disciplines do you most need to address? Of these, which ones should you implement first? Remember, these are only some means of abiding in Christ. If you try to make spiritual discipline your Christ, you will wither like a branch cut from the vine. The spiritual disciplines are only ways of connecting with Christ and receiving from him the grace to walk worthy of his holy name so that we increasingly produce more fruit.

Conclusion

Let us seek wisdom from God, and the Spirit's grace, in order to turn knowledge into practice, for we do not truly know anything until it is translated into action. Thomas Cartwright (1535-1603) said, 'A man knows so much of Christianity as he practiseth.'[75]

We must remember, too, that Christian practice is in essence becoming a humble servant to others, even if everything in us rebels at the thought. R. C. Sproul tells how he experienced servitude holding down a summer job as a seminary student. His job required him to sweep up cigarette butts and other litter in the parking lots outside a dormitory for nursing students. When some students walked by, he greeted them only to find them turning up their noses and ignoring him. He wanted to protest, saying, 'Wait! I'm a college graduate. You are just in nurses' school. You don't understand the pecking order here.' The Lord convicted him then and there that he was a follower of Christ, who was not only a servant but was upset when he was treated like one.[76]

It is challenging to grow in Christ's pattern and in pleasing God. That's why we need the spiritual disciplines. Thanks be to God, he has given us many ways to apply the Word and prayer to our lives, not just in private disciplines but also in the family, church, and neighborly relationships.

Just as an athlete who disciplines himself to train that he might win a gold medal, so we must keep our hope fixed on Christ by using the spiritual disciplines. Growing in obedience has gracious, eternal rewards. Do we truly believe that God will reward our obedience, as Jesus taught us? Do we truly believe that every act of obedience gains heavenly treasure, and every sin loses a reward that we might have had?

Robert Murray M'Cheyne (1813-1843) said, 'I have no doubt that every sin, inconsistency, backsliding, and decay of God's children takes away something from their eternal glory. It is a loss for all eternity; and the more fully and unreservedly we follow the Lord Jesus now, the more abundant will our entrance be into His everlasting kingdom. The closer we walk with Christ now, the closer will we walk with Him to all eternity.'[77]

Let us then follow the Lord fully. Let us be like Caleb, the son of Jephunneh, who followed the Lord fully; and press on to receive a full reward from our gracious Master.

3

Spiritual growth in experience

For this cause we also, since the day we heard it, do not cease to pray for you, and to desire that ye might be … strengthened with all might, according to his glorious power, unto all patience and longsuffering with joyfulness; giving thanks unto the Father, which hath made us meet to be partakers of the inheritance of the saints in light: who hath delivered us from the power of darkness, and hath translated us into the kingdom of his dear Son: in whom we have redemption through his blood, even the forgiveness of sins
(Colossians 1:9, 11-14).

John Bunyan (1628-1688) had been led through conviction of sin and fear of damnation to a basic morality of life and religious devotion. He was walking through town one day and heard some women talking about the things of God. Being 'a brisk talker' himself in things of religion, Bunyan was nonetheless shaken by what he heard. He wrote:

> I heard, but I understood not; for they were far above, out of my reach; for their talk was about a new birth, the work of God on their hearts, also how they were convinced of their miserable state by nature; they talked how God had visited their souls with his love in the Lord Jesus, and with what words and promises they had been refreshed, comforted, and supported against the temptations of the devil… They also discoursed of their own wretchedness of heart, of their unbelief; and did contemn, slight, and abhor their own righteousness, as filthy and insufficient to do them any good.
>
> And methought they spake as if joy did make them speak; they spake with such pleasantness of Scriptural language, and with such appearance of grace in all they said, that they were to me, as if they had found a new world.[78]

The world these women had found was not that of mere Christian doctrine but of Christian experience. This realm is unknown to the unbeliever, no matter how religious he may seem. Thankfully, God later brought Bunyan into this new world so that he, too, experienced the joy of it. It moved him to speak and write of God's ways with the soul. Let us now turn to the matter of spiritual growth in personal experience of the truth and power of the gospel.

This chapter concludes our consideration of spiritual growth, according to Colossians 1:9-14. In the first chapter, I discussed spiritual growth in knowledge. We looked at growing in the knowledge of God's saving plan in the Son ('filled with the knowledge of his will'), which is written on the heart by the Holy Spirit ('in all wisdom and spiritual understanding'), and results in a deepening knowledge of God the Father ('increasing in the knowledge of God').

In the second chapter, I focused on spiritual growth in practice. We learned that divine knowledge aims at us growing in Jesus Christ's pattern of humility ('that ye might walk worthy of the Lord'), growing in pleasing God ('unto all pleasing'), and growing in spiritual fruitfulness ('being fruitful in every good work'). We talked about the practical methods of abiding in Christ so that we might be fruitful. The way to do that is to make use of the means of grace, that is, the spiritual disciplines of using the Word and prayer in our private, family, church, and community activities.

Now, let us examine spiritual growth in experience, drawing from Colossians 1:11-14. In these verses we see two main areas of spiritual experience: divine power and human gratitude. There are, of course, many other areas of spiritual growth that could be addressed experientially, but we will confine ourselves to these two as they are drawn from the text.

Grow in the experience of God's power

Having prayed for the Colossian Christians to be filled
with knowledge so they might walk worthy of the Lord,
Paul describes what that walk should look like. He uses four
participial phrases to do this. The first two phrases (in v. 10)
described a life of fruitful activity and deepening knowledge
of the heavenly Father. Now we consider the third phrase
which shows us another aspect of the walk or way of life
that flows out of a growing knowledge of Christ, namely,
the experience of God's power at work in us.

Colossians 1:11 speaks of being 'strengthened with all
might, according to his glorious power, unto all patience
and longsuffering with joyfulness'. The gospel is not just
a philosophy or set of ideas; it is 'the power of God unto
salvation to every one that believeth' (Rom. 1:16). Such
power is necessary because the Christian is involved in
constant warfare against the world, the flesh and the devil.
We have work to do, battles to fight, trials to endure, and
crosses to bear. Surely what is expected of us far exceeds
our own resources. We need access to a greater power,
which God promises when he says, 'As thy days, so shall
thy strength be' (Deut. 33:25).

Growing from babes to young men to fathers in grace

God's intent is that believers in Christ grow from 'little

children' to 'young men' to 'fathers' in the faith, as the apostle John writes (see 1 John 2:12-14). John Newton (1725-1807) called these the stages of desiring, conflict and contemplation.[79] New Christians are 'little children' in Christ. Their experience of God and salvation in Christ is fresh and vivid (1 John 2:12a, 13c), and they are full of holy desires and affections. At a later stage they become 'young men' in the Lord, who have grown in their knowledge of the Word, and learned how to fight against the world, the flesh and the devil. Thus 1 John 2:14b says, 'I have written unto you, young men, because ye are strong, and the word of God abideth in you, and ye have overcome the wicked one.' Yet later, they may become fathers in the faith through more wholehearted surrender and contemplation of God by beholding the glory of the Father in the face of Jesus Christ.

Paul wants the Colossian believers to grow up spiritually. Like John, he wants to see them growing from infancy to youth, from little children to young men, and from young men to fathers.

Being strengthened for every need

Paul prayed for converts to be 'strengthened with all might'. When Paul wrote '*all* might' he did not mean infinite power. God alone is almighty. The 'all' here means power sufficient for all the tasks at hand. Philippians 4:13 says,

'I can do all things through Christ which strengtheneth me.' Christians are to grow into a well-rounded, holistic maturity in which they experience the sufficiency of Christ in every need. John Davenant (1572-1641) listed five actions that require power from God: (1) doing good works, however difficult; (2) striving against sin; (3) despising earthly things; (4) resisting temptation; and (5) enduring affliction.[80] He quoted the church father Cyprian to remind us that we need comprehensive strength to face our comprehensive battle against sin, saying, 'If avarice [or greed] be overthrown, lust rises; if lust be subdued, ambition succeeds; if ambition is spurned, wrath incenses, pride inflates, etc.'[81]

How much strength is needed? Ultimately, that need not be measured in human terms, because the might Paul speaks of is to be measured 'according to his glorious power'. The preposition 'according to' sets up a standard of comparison. In other words, in God's 'glorious power', that is, the infinite power by which God does such glorious things (Ps. 72:1, 19), we can find all the strength that we need.

This power flows from heaven to earth because as Christians, we are members of Christ,[82] brought into union with him by the power of the Spirit. Thus Paul writes in Ephesians 6:10: 'Be strong in the Lord, and in the power of his might.' The same Spirit who dwells in the God-man now seated at the Father's right hand also dwells in us (Rom. 8:11). According to Davenant: 'The strengthening power is the Holy Spirit himself, with his gifts; who breathes wonderful might into our infirm minds.'[83]

Learning to lean on God's power alone

We grow spiritually as we cease striving in our own strength and rely more and more on the Spirit's power. Every Christian must learn to wait upon the Lord who 'giveth power to the faint, and to them that have no might he increaseth strength. Even the youths shall faint and be weary, and the young men shall utterly fall: but they that wait upon the LORD shall renew their strength; they shall mount up with wings as eagles; they shall run, and not be weary; and they shall walk, and not faint' (Isa. 40:29–31).

Learning to wait on the Lord, putting our hope in him alone, not in ourselves or any other creature, is essential to spiritual growth. We learn this lesson very slowly, for it goes against the grain of our pride. We must die daily to ourselves and continually look to Jesus. Newton wrote:

Neither has [the mature believer], properly speaking, any more strength or stock of grace inherent in himself than [the growing believer], or even than [the new convert]. He is in the same state of absolute dependence, as incapable of performing spiritual

acts, or of resisting temptations by his own power, as
he was at the first day of his setting out. Yet in a sense
he is much stronger, because he has a more feeling
and constant sense of his own weakness… Thus he
is strong, not in himself, but in the grace that is in
Christ Jesus.[84]

Our heavenly Father wisely disciplines us to drive us out
of self-sufficiency so that we lean on his strength alone.
The ministry of the Word is fraught with discouragements
and trials because God presses us beyond our strength, so
that we do not trust in ourselves but in God, who raises
the dead (2 Cor. 1:9). Paul said in 2 Corinthians 4:8-10,
'We are troubled on every side, yet not distressed; we are
perplexed, but not in despair; persecuted, but not forsaken;
cast down, but not destroyed; always bearing about in
the body the dying of the Lord Jesus, that the life also
of Jesus might be made manifest in our body.' We must
live in communion with Christ. In the fellowship of his
sufferings we come to know the power of his resurrection.

If your aim as a minister is to put your own abilities on
display, you are striving against God. Work for excellence
out of love for his name, but also accept the limitations he
imposes upon you according to his will. Paul writes in 2
Corinthians 12 of his thorn in the flesh. We don't know
what it was. Perhaps it was a physical problem such as
weakness in his voice or eye, or a chronic or degenerative
illness such as malaria or gout. Perhaps the thorn was a

person who dogged him with accusations, criticisms, or threats. Three times Paul asked God to remove this thorn. It is good to pray for deliverance, but in Paul's case, the Lord's answer was, 'My grace is sufficient for thee: for my strength is made perfect in weakness' (v. 9).

Are you willing to live in weakness? Can you glory in your infirmities? It may seem strange, but Paul's prayer for us to be 'strengthened with all might, according to his glorious power', is answered not by prosperity or success, but in the midst of troubles, failures and sorrows. Christ often conquers us through a cross of suffering.

In time we learn that Christ meant what he said, 'Without me ye can do nothing' (John 15:5). We cannot so much as move without his will and assistance. God's power is at work even when we least expect it, or are least aware of it. God gives us strength at the point of our greatest weakness. 'Weak and heavy laden, cumbered with a load of care,' we nonetheless find the strength to rise up and go forward, and to press on in the way. We may feel like a seed planted in a rock, with no room to grow, but God may still use us to break the rock!

Paul writes in Colossians 1:28-29 of the heavy demands of the ministry, and how he found the strength he needed by looking to Christ: 'Whom we preach, warning every man, and teaching every man in all wisdom; that we may present every man perfect in Christ Jesus: whereunto I also labour, striving according to his working, which worketh in me mightily.' He also said in 1 Corinthians 15:10, 'But by the grace of God I am what I am: and his grace which was bestowed upon me was not in vain; but I labored more abundantly than they all: yet not I, but the grace of God which was with me.'

The supply of God's power and grace may vary in different seasons of ministry. Just as there are seasons in farming, so there are seasons in church ministry. God determines what those seasons are in your labors; whether they are times of plowing, planting, tending, waiting or reaping. Christ said in John 4:37-38, 'And herein is that saying true, One soweth, and another reapeth. I sent you to reap that whereon ye bestowed no labor: other men labored, and ye are entered into their labors.' God may call you to sow but leave the reaping to someone else. Does that mean God's power was not active in your ministry? Of course not; how can others reap if you do not sow?

Seasons of plowing are necessary to break up hard soil before it is ready to receive seed. It takes back-breaking labor to remove rocks and stumps from a field before it is ready for plowing. It is not up to you to determine what season you and your church are in. Whether God calls you to pull up stumps, plow, plant, cultivate, reap, or some combination of them, do everything you are called to do in his power.

Learning patience, longsuffering and joyfulness

Colossians 1:11 identifies the particular needs that are supplied by God's power at work in us. God strengthens us 'unto all patience and longsuffering with joyfulness'. In other words, this power does not allow us to ride along like triumphant conquerors at the head of a parade. Rather, this power is given, not to rescue us from all our troubles, but to enable us to press forward in the way, bearing the heat of the day, even if our hearts are broken and our souls are weary.

'Patience' is endurance, or the ability to go in the right direction and to stand firm despite weakness, opposition, fear, obstacles, pain, disappointments and discouragement.[85] Note once more, that Paul says, 'all patience', meaning the patience to endure all things. 'Long-suffering' is the strength to suffer wrongs and provocations from others, responding with love and forgiveness, instead of anger and vengeance.[86] So 'patience and longsuffering' are needed by those who suffer trials and conflicts, in order to persevere in faith and obedience.

This is not the bitter, hardened perseverance of a stoic. It is not sheer grit, or a grim resolve to do one's duty. The patience and longsuffering are entwined together with joyfulness, in a threefold cord, not easily broken. Such joy is essential in the Christian life. The *Heidelberg Catechism*

(Q. 90) says that 'the quickening of the new man' is 'a sincere joy of heart in God, through Christ, and with love and delight to live according to the will of God in all good works'.[87] Therefore spiritual growth includes increasing in our joy in God through Christ, and growing delight in our duties, for in our duties God meets with us.

Nehemiah 8:10 says, 'The joy of the LORD is your strength.' This joy sustains us in the face of many trials. When our enemies prevail, crops fail, our cattle perish, our stores are exhausted, and our efforts collapse, believers still joy in God and find strength in him: 'Yet I will rejoice in the LORD, I will joy in the God of my salvation. The LORD God is my strength, and he will make my feet like hinds' feet, and he will make me to walk upon mine high places' (Hab. 3:18-19).

We return again to the joy of knowing God. Our strength to obey and to serve comes from knowing God in a way that fills our souls with joy. Daniel 11:32 says, 'The people that do know their God shall be strong, and do exploits.'

Never underestimate the strength God can give you in times of weakness. Russell and Darlene Deibler were serving as missionaries in Indonesia when World War II erupted. Captured by the Axis forces, both went to prison, and Russell died there. For almost four years, Darlene was held in the Kempeitai prison, which was infamous for torture and death. She remained in solitary confinement in a six- by six-foot cell with a boarded-up window. She was being slowly starved to death on a meager diet of rice. Disease wracked her body. But Darlene found refuge in the Scriptures she had memorized. When her captors interrogated her, accused her of being an American spy, and beat her, Darlene was comforted by 2 Corinthians 12:9: 'My grace is sufficient for thee.' She also found joy in singing these words:

When we have exhausted our store of endurance,
And our strength has failed ere the day is half done,
When we reach the end of our hoarded resources,
The Father's full giving is only begun.
His love has no limit, His grace has no measure.
His power has no boundary known unto men.
For out of His infinite riches in Jesus,
He giveth and giveth and giveth again.[88]

The Lord was with Darlene in that prison cell just as he was with Joseph in an Egyptian jail. The Lord is with all of his people in all their trials to preserve them and help them to endure. Let us examine three practical steps that we can we take, by the Spirit's grace, to obtain the promise of strength to endure, by the power of God.

1. Be honest about your weaknesses. As Christians, and especially as leaders, we may find it difficult to admit that we are weak, especially in regard to the duties and requisite skills of our calling. We don't want to think about such weakness, and we certainly don't want to talk about it. We should be discreet about when and where to talk with others about our weaknesses and failures. There are some Christians who seem to enjoy giving sensational accounts of their past sins. We don't want to be hypochondriacs, either, who broadcast every ache and pain to win others' sympathy or excuse our own laziness.

However, much of our reluctance to talk honestly about our weaknesses comes from pride. We desperately want to appear strong in the eyes of others. We fear they will think less of us if we admit to any weakness. But such pretense — for that is what it is — is ridiculous. People can see through the pretense. We are only deceiving ourselves. So cultivate humility and honesty about your weaknesses. Remember that 'God resisteth the proud, but giveth grace unto the humble' (James 4:6).

2. Look to Christ habitually for strength and joy. Get in the habit of thinking expectantly about Christ's ability to supply all your needs. In Ephesians 1, Paul prayed that believers would know the exceeding greatness of God's power towards them. Then he launched into a description of Christ's exaltation to God's right hand in the heavens, far above all earthly powers (Eph. 1:19-23). Why did he do that? He wanted to draw us upward by looking at God's power through the Lord Jesus.

So, each morning, look to Christ and consider his immense ability to help you with anything you will do that day. Don't just call on him in emergencies; look to Christ every day. Anticipate tasks and temptations before they arise, and fix your eyes on the Author and Finisher of your faith. Christ is near at hand, ready to help; he is at no time absent from you, but abides with you in his godhead, majesty, grace and Spirit (*Heidelberg Catechism*, Lord's Day 18). He is both able and willing to exercise his power through you for the tearing down of strongholds and leading every thought captive to Christ.

Above all, look to Christ as your joy. When a prominent Christian leader recently came to the end of his life, he said, 'I have spent much of my life seeing Christ as useful. I wish that I had spent more of my life seeing Christ as beautiful.' Rejoice in the Lord. Exercise your soul to rejoice in him again and again. Do not merely draw power from him to get things done. Love him and delight in him as your life.

3. Pray without ceasing. Call upon the Father to supply all your needs out of his glorious riches in Christ Jesus. Pray for strength for yourself and for others. In your weakness, cry out to the Holy Spirit. Pour out your heart to the Lord. Bring all your anxieties to Christ, then seek the power of his peace to guard your heart. Mingle praises with your tears, and songs with your cries for mercy. Mute rejoicing is joy tied up and gagged. So sing to the Lord a new song!

The more you cultivate honesty about your weakness, have faith in Christ's strength, pray for God's provision, and rejoice in the Lord in the midst of your trials, the more you will grow in experiencing God's power. This is the first aspect of growing in Christian experience.

Grow in the experience of gratitude

Colossians 1:12 offers the fourth participial phrase of our text which describes the growing Christian as one who is ever 'giving thanks unto the Father, which hath made us meet to be partakers of the inheritance of the saints in light'.[89] Gratitude is the heartbeat of growth. In expanding the idea of being filled with the Spirit, Paul said in Ephesians 5:20 that growth aims at, and results in, 'giving thanks always for all things unto God and the Father in the name of our Lord Jesus Christ'.

The Heidelberg Catechism (Q. 86) says, 'Christ, having redeemed and delivered us by His blood, also renews us by His Holy Spirit after His own image; that so we may testify, by the whole of our conduct, our gratitude to God for His blessings.'

Gratitude is our response to God's grace. When someone says 'grace' at a meal, he is acknowledging God's grace in providing food and drink.[90] If someone pays you what he owes you, that does not inspire much gratitude. But an undeserved gift, freely given, reveals the heart of a beautiful, generous person. God's gift of his Son for our salvation is a revelation of the greatness of his love toward us (John 3:16). In 2 Corinthians 9:15, Paul expresses the gratitude that every Christian should feel, saying, 'Thanks be unto God for his unspeakable gift.'[91]

Gratitude is our response of love to the loveliness we discover in God as 'the overflowing fountain of all good'.[92] True gratitude is more than saying thanks; it is an expression of love. We love God because he first loved us (1 John 4:19). In gratitude we do not merely love God for his gifts, but for what his gifts tell us about him. John Owen said, 'When the soul sees God, in his dispensation of love, to be love, to be infinitely lovely and loving, rests upon and delights in him as such — then it hath communion with him in love.'[93]

Gratitude to God is the bond and debt of worship and service, because God's grace reveals his glory as God. His gifts bind us with the sacred obligation to give ourselves back to him as living sacrifices (Rom. 12:1). He made us; we should glorify him as our Creator (Rom. 1:21). He has redeemed us in Christ, and we should glorify him as the God of our salvation.

Our gratitude is directed to God the Father (Col. 1:3; 3:17), for his grace reveals his fatherly, adoptive, compassionate love for us. The Father blessed us with every spiritual blessing in Christ (Eph. 1:3). The Father chose us in Christ before time began (Eph. 1:4). The Father predestined dead sinners to become his adopted children through Christ (Eph. 1:5). The Father sent his Son to become a man to redeem us (Gal. 4:4-5). The Father sent his Spirit into our hearts as the Spirit of adoption (Gal. 4:6). The vision of God as our Father is the heart of his revelation to us in Christ. Thus God the Father is the focal point of our gratitude.

Colossians 1:12 specifically talks about our gratitude to 'the Father, which hath made us meet to be partakers of the inheritance of the saints in light'. This gratitude arises from hope, for we now have a future. We may expect happiness and wholeness because God the Father has saved us. We are no longer outsiders, aliens and enemies but beloved children and heirs of the kingdom of God. We will share in the 'light', that is, the radiance of his glory that fills heaven today like the sun fills the world beneath with light. One day the knowledge of the glory of God will fill the earth 'as the waters cover the sea' (Isa. 11:9).

God's grace 'hath made us meet', that is, given us the right, as his children and heirs, to enjoy our inheritance.[94] Writing to a Gentile audience, Paul affirms that the Gentile believers are entitled to the same rights and privileges of Jewish believers, for all are the children of God in Christ. Such a redemption is the act of almighty power, performed by God's omnipotence.[95] So Paul prayed for the knowledge of God's grace to fill us to overflowing with gratitude.

The following three clauses in Colossians 1:12-14 describe the basis for our gratitude in ways that relate to our misery and deliverance as well as to the three-fold office of Christ. As Gerard Wisse (1873-1957) explained so well, each of the three offices of Christ touch our knowledge of misery, deliverance and gratitude.[96] In this last chapter we will explore only some aspects of Christ's wonderful ministry in the elect.

As we look at this text, you might say, 'I thought that Paul was praying for spiritual growth. Why is he rehearsing the gospel?' The answer is that growth in gratitude springs from our experiential knowledge of the gospel of Christ. Spiritual growth comes through the Holy Spirit blessing experiential preaching and experiential meditation on fundamental gospel truths.

Misery, gratitude, and Christ our Prophet

Colossians 1:13 says we must give thanks unto the Father 'who hath delivered us from the power of darkness'. As he did in Ephesians 2, Paul reminds us of what we once were (Eph. 2:1, 11-12). Our gratitude for deliverance flows out of remembering the greatness of our misery without Christ. He who is forgiven much loves much (Luke 7:42-

43, 47). One reason for the profound ingratitude of many people today is their shallow view of their sin and misery. They have no sense of the 'exceeding sinfulness of sin'.

Therefore the Holy Spirit calls us to contemplate our sin and misery. We once lived in 'darkness'. When you were a child, darkness transformed the familiar contents of your bedroom into a hall of horrors. In wartime, enemies can attack under cover of darkness to slaughter you. Thieves break in at night. Wild animals prowl at night in search of helpless victims.

But the darkness Paul refers to is a darkness of the mind, heart and will. Ephesians 4:18 said, 'Having the understanding darkened, being alienated from the life of God through the ignorance that is in them, because of the blindness of their heart'. In the darkness of our fallen condition, we could not see spiritual light because we hated spiritual life and loved the darkness of our evil deeds (John 3:19-20).

As sinners we were enslaved to 'the power of darkness', ruling over us as a kingdom or dominion (literally 'authority').[97] Paul says in 2 Corinthians 4:3-4, 'But if our gospel be hid, it is hid to them that are lost: in whom the god of this world hath blinded the minds of them which believe not, lest the light of the glorious gospel of Christ, who is the image of God, should shine unto them.' How hopeless our condition was, when Satan led us forth as prisoners, with our feet in chains and our eyes blindfolded, towards the precipice of hell! Generation after generation fell into the pit. Yet we followed Satan willingly, fulfilling the desires of the flesh and of the mind (Eph. 2:2-3). We were tied with the chains forged by our own will and understanding.

The Father has rescued us from this doom. We did not save ourselves; we did not even meet him halfway. We didn't even lift a finger. We could do nothing because we were dead in sin. The Father sent his Son to be the Light of the world. The light of heaven came to earth and became flesh (John 1:9, 14). Today the light of heaven comes to each elect soul and regenerates him, making him a new creature in Christ. Paul said in 2 Corinthians 4:6, 'For God, who commanded the light to shine out of darkness, hath shined in our hearts, to give the light of the knowledge of the glory of God in the face of Jesus Christ.' This new creation is as glorious as the first creation, when God said, 'Let there be light.'

The Father saved us by sending Christ as our Prophet. In his prophetic ministry, Christ instructs us outwardly by the Spirit-inspired Word, and illuminates us inwardly by the Spirit-applied Word. You are no longer a slave under the dominion of darkness because Christ opened your mind to understand the Scriptures (*cf*. Luke 24:45). Christ opened your mind to receive the fullness of grace and truth that is in him (John 1:16-17; Eph. 4:21). Wisse said, 'This divine instruction penetrates the intellect deeply — very deeply. This penetration is so deep that the very depths of the soul are touched by Him who alone is wisdom. Thus … Christ gives us an internal knowledge that touches the heart.'[98]

Many people are overwhelmed by wonder when they first put on eyeglasses or corrective lenses to improve their vision. They put on the glasses, and — wonder of wonders — they can see each leaf on the tree as the wind moved it. They could read signs! They had a newfound joy and appreciation for the funny frames of metal, plastic and glass hanging on people's noses. Imagine what it was like for the blind man who was given sight by Jesus. The arguments of the Pharisees bounced like rubber balls off the granite wall of his simple testimony, 'whereas I was blind, now I see' (John 9:25).

How much more amazing, then, is the gift of spiritual sight. For years and years we were blind, and went on blindly through life not knowing the God who made us, but sinning against him every day, heedless of the danger that awaited us at life's end. Now, by the light of Scripture we can see beyond this earth into heaven itself, where Christ appears in all his glory and beauty, seated at the right hand of God.

The more you understand the necessity and power of Christ's prophetic ministry, the more grateful you will be to the Father. We tend to be proud of our understanding, for, as 1 Corinthians 8:1 says, 'Knowledge puffeth up.' We compare ourselves to others. We look down on people who seem to have far less doctrinal insight. But when we do, we show that we are blind to what God has given us as a free gift of grace, for what do we have that we have not received?

May God remind us daily of our former state under the power of darkness, and fill us with gratitude for our rescue. As we better understand the power of darkness, we will recognize the remaining fragments of darkness that oppress our souls. These spiritual blind spots will humble us and make us grateful to Christ.

Deliverance, gratitude, and Christ our King

In Colossians 1:13, Paul also prayed for gratitude because the Father 'hath translated us into the kingdom of his dear Son'. Gratitude is produced not only by knowing what we are saved *from*, but also what we are saved *for*. The verb 'translate' communicates a change of citizenship as well as a removal from the authority of one kingdom and placement under a new jurisdiction.[99] We thus have a new identity as citizens of the kingdom of heaven. We have a new King, live under a new law, and owe nothing to the realm and ruler we have left behind. We have a place in the new creation where God will restore all things and leave nothing under a curse. Is this not reason to be thankful?

We are now participants in the kingdom of God's Son. God gave us to his Son (John 6:37). He placed us in Christ's kingdom, not by moving us from one geographic location to another, but wresting us from Satan's grasp and placing us under the power of Christ our King.

Paul said in Colossians 1:15-17, '[He] is the image of the invisible God, the firstborn of every creature: for by him were all things created, that are in heaven, and that are in earth, visible and invisible, whether they be thrones, or dominions, or principalities, or powers: all things were created by him, and for him: and he is before all things, and by him all things consist.' Christ reveals the divine nature with infinite glory, has a mediatorial kingship over all creation, reigning over all things in heaven and earth as the firstborn Son of the Father. 'Firstborn' does not mean the first one created, but, in accord with its Old Testament usage, means having preeminent authority over the inheritance (Ps. 89:27).

But the Father has also given his Son the throne of David, to rule over the people of God as Head of the church. Paul describes this in Colossians 1:18, saying, 'He is the head of the body, the church: who is the beginning, the firstborn from the dead; that in all things he might have the preeminence.' Thus Christ is the incarnate image of God, the last Adam at the head of a new humanity raised out of our sin and misery. At the core of this work is Christ's possession of us (Titus 2:14). He will have 'preeminence', as 'the head of the body' who conquers and rules us with infinite authority, that we may be his people and possession for ever.

Wisse wrote of Christ: 'As resurrected king He is fully and entirely authorized to demand and bring about the deliverance of His redeemed ones.'[100] Christ establishes his throne in our hearts so that we are willing in the day of his power. He added: 'We become a distinctive people with a distinctive King and a distinctive law... Therefore, as King He will lay claim to His lawful possession... They must not only come into heaven, but they must also become the battalions of Christ — His people and soldiers. They must become kings and priests themselves.'[101] Christ commissions us as his royal servants to establish his kingdom on earth. Wisse said, 'God speaks, and we in turn as kings are the instrument whereby the stamp of God's dominion is placed upon His creation.'[102]

Belonging to Christ's kingdom enriches us beyond human comprehension. The Father unites us with his royal Son in this kingdom so that we might share in all his blessings (1 Cor. 1:30). Romans 14:17 says, 'For the kingdom of God is not meat and drink; but righteousness, and peace, and joy in the Holy Ghost.' In being joined to the supreme Image of God, we are being transformed into the glorious image of God (Col. 3:10). His fullness as Lord over all fills us up and overflows us (Col. 2:9-10). Davenant wrote: 'By the kingdom of Christ we understand all the benefits of grace which are obtained through union with and subjection to Christ our spiritual King.'[103] Today we share by faith in the life of this King, and when he appears we will share in his glory (Col. 3:3-4). We are in Christ and Christ is in us so that we share in this glorious hope, of which Paul said in Colossians 1:27, 'Christ in you, the hope of glory'. Though we are weak and poverty-stricken in ourselves, Christ has become power and riches to us beyond all measure. Let us give thanks to the Father for his indescribable gift!

Our gratitude to the Father increases as we increasingly value his Son. If we have shallow views of Christ, our gratitude will be of little weight. It will be easily overwhelmed by the troubles of this life, and we will complain. But when we see that God has given us such a wondrous King and kingdom, we say in amazement, 'Whom have I in heaven but thee? And there is none upon earth that I desire beside thee' (Ps. 73:25). Owen wrote that we may then 'value Christ above all other things and persons... Christ and a dungeon, Christ and a cross, is infinitely sweeter than a crown, a scepter without him... They value him above their lives... It is known what is reported of Ignatius when he was led to martyrdom: "Let what will," said he, "come upon me, only so I may obtain Jesus Christ."'[104] Treasuring Christ is the wellspring of our gratitude.

Our King is described in Colossians 1:13 as 'his dear Son', literally, 'the Son of his love'. This unique expression communicates the Father's boundless delight and eternal love for his perfect Son.[105] Solomon, the royal son of David, was named 'Jedidiah', meaning the 'beloved of the LORD' (2 Sam. 12:25). Likewise Christ, the ultimate son of David, is beloved of the Father beyond human expression. The most devoted, proud and tender love that any earthly father feels for his child is only the faintest shadow of God's love for his Son. Christ is the Jedidiah *par excellence*. John Eadie wrote: 'He is the object of boundless and unchanging affection… The love of God to one who is His own Image will be in harmony with the Divine nature of both — infinite as its object, and eternal and majestic.'[106]

We have a share in a kingdom that cannot fail, for the zeal of the Lord of hosts guarantees it (Isa. 9:7). Every ounce of the Father's infinite glory is committed to honoring his Son. We are not mere spectators cheering on the Son as he experiences his Father's love for him. The Father's love for his Son overflows to us as well (John 17:23). Because Christ is all for us and in us, we too, being in Christ as our Savior and Elder Brother, are 'holy and beloved' to God (Col. 3:12). We are regarded as sons by God's grace (Eph. 1:5; Gal. 4:5). The Spirit of adoption is sent into our hearts crying, 'Abba, Father' (Gal. 4:6; Rom. 8:15), and enables us to say, 'I am the LORD's' (Isa. 44:3-5). How great our privileges are in Christ!

When the Father transferred us out of the power of darkness into the kingdom of his Son, he gave us abundant cause to thank him for ever. This is the best rags-to-riches story ever written — and it is our story! But we will only be moved to gratitude to the extent that we know these things on an experiential level — that is, we experience, we taste, and we are overwhelmed by what God does for us in his Son. As long as what God does for sinners in Christ remains mere ideas flitting about in our brains, they will mean little to us. But these truths, when experienced in the depth of our soul, ignite us into a blazing fire of love for our Savior.

The grace of the king arouses gratitude. Mephibosheth, the son of Jonathan, was unable to walk because he was dropped as a infant (2 Sam. 4:4). After the house of Saul fell under God's judgement and David became king, Mephibosheth lost his inheritance. He could have lost his life as well, for it was common for a new king to kill the family of his predecessor to eliminate potential rivals. God later revealed that the house of Saul was cursed because Saul had murdered the Gibeonites (2 Sam. 21:1-6). But David, keeping his covenant with his friend Jonathan, son of Saul, restored the lands of Saul to Mephibosheth, gave him servants to farm the land, and invited him to eat at the king's table (2 Sam. 9:1-13; 21:7).

Mephibosheth was overwhelmed with gratitude. David had elevated him from a landless cripple in a cursed family to a prince. He bowed down and exclaimed: 'What is thy servant, that thou shouldest look upon such a dead dog as I am?' (2 Sam. 9:8). When David's wicked son Absalom forced David to flee from his palace, Mephibosheth so loved his king that he did not care for his feet or trim his beard or wash his clothes, but publicly grieved until David returned to power (2 Sam. 19:24). No doubt this did not win favor with Absalom and his friends. When David returned to the palace, Mephibosheth did not care whether he got his lands and honor back; he just loved his king (2 Sam. 19:29-30).

If this was the gratitude that Mephibosheth showed to King David, how much more should we offer thanksgiving and love to God for our King, Jesus Christ? We were once crippled by sin. Our first father, Adam, forfeited our inheritance and brought us under a curse. We were more unclean to God than the rotting corpse of a dog was to a strict Jew. But our King was faithful to his covenant obligation, and restored our inheritance. He says to us, 'Sit with me at my table.' We should be overwhelmed with gratitude for such a King. We should love him regardless of what the world thinks and be grieved every day by the way men dishonor Christ.

The church needs experiential preaching to promote our gratitude to God for Jesus Christ. Experiential preaching addresses the vital matter of how a Christian experiences the truth of biblical, Calvinistic doctrine in his life.[107] Through experiential preaching, God establishes the throne of Christ in the hearts of his elect. Too often preachers neglect the truth and fall into emotionalism, or they neglect experience and promote cold orthodoxy (which is not orthodoxy at all). In the Reformed understanding, experiential preaching brings together the dry kindling and seasoned wood of God's truth with the flame of love so that, if the Spirit is pleased to blow upon it, a warm fire of vital godliness is ignited in listeners.

Since Reformed experiential preaching is crucial for cultivating gratitude, let me briefly explain what it means. This may help guide your own preaching and your prayers for God to raise up more men who preach like this.

1. Reformed experiential preachers expound the Bible. They do not build experientialism upon human notions; they 'preach the Word' (2 Tim. 4:2) with sound exegetical and hermeneutical principles. They derive their content from specific texts or passages of Scripture. In Colossians 1:9, Paul reminds us that spiritual growth begins with being filled with the knowledge of God's will.

2. Reformed experiential preachers proclaim Christ. They do not merely lecture on the words and grammar of a text. They do not merely recite confessions of faith. They herald Christ as the Scriptures reveal him and as the confessions reflect that revelation. The great theme of experiential preaching is Jesus Christ, for he is the supreme focus, prism and goal of God's revelation.[108] Spiritual growth builds upon the knowledge of who Christ is and what he has done as our Prophet, Priest and King.

3. Reformed experiential preachers make application to the heart. Robert Burns said, 'Christianity should not only be known, and understood, and believed, but also felt, and enjoyed, and practically applied.'[109] 'The Westminster Directory for the Publick Worship of God' said the preacher 'is not to rest in general doctrine, although never so much cleared and confirmed, but to bring it home to special use, by application to his hearers … in such a manner, that his auditors may feel the word of God to be quick and powerful, and a discerner of the thoughts and intents of the heart'. It went on to say that these applications were to include *instruction* in truth, *confutation* of false doctrines endangering the flock, *exhortation* of men to duty with helpful means, *admonition* against sin in its misery and danger, *comfort* with answers to the doubting soul's objections, and *self-examination* for graces and sins.[110] We would add the application of *doxology,* which leads people to extol the glory of God as revealed in a particular text.

4. Reformed experiential preachers discriminate spiritually. While racial discrimination is an abomination to the God who created all men of one blood (Acts 17:26), the Bible continually discriminates or distinguishes between the saved and the unsaved. Thus preaching must clearly discriminate between the world and the visible church, between the hypocrite in the church and the true believer, and between immature and mature believers. Paul showed the contrast between the power of darkness and the kingdom of God's dear Son in describing the growth of the converted.

5. Reformed experiential preachers speak with realism, faithfulness and optimism. Such preaching is realistic because it explains how things go for Christians (Rom. 7:14-25). This preaching is realistic in speaking of our triumphs as well as our frustrations and failures. It is faithful in explaining how matters ought to go in the Christian life (Rom. 8:1-27). And it is optimistic in explaining how matters ultimately will go for Christians (Rom. 8:28-39). Our great hope and confidence is in our sovereign Savior.

6. Reformed experiential preachers maintain a balanced Christianity. Their preaching balances the objective and the subjective, knowing that the proclamation of objective truth should always aim for a subjective response, and the subjective experience must be understood in the light of objective truth. It distinguishes between Christ's work *for* us and Christ's work *in* us, but never separates them from each other. It balances God's sovereignty and man's responsibility, offering both in biblical proportion.

7. Reformed experiential preachers walk in holiness. They do not merely preach Christ as King; they obey Christ as King. They are single-minded men who fear the Lord rather than human beings. They value a good name, that is, a reputation for godliness and uprightness of life, but disdain popularity. They strive to win their hearers' consciences but not their applause. They sincerely love the men, women and children whom they serve. They are gospel men through and through, meaning that in all their labors, private and public, they look to Christ and depend on the Holy Spirit. They know they are unable to do a single good work or open a single heart apart from the grace of Christ. They are men of 'true faith, firm hope, and ardent love'.[111]

In short, our text in Colossians shows that Christian growth depends on an *experiential* knowledge of Christ. A church may be well informed about how God delivered us from darkness and transferred us into Christ's kingdom, yet remain barren of love for the King. We need Reformed experiential preachers through whom the Good Shepherd speaks to his sheep and calls them by name into the rich pastures of his grace. We need heralds of the King of kings.

So far we have looked at spiritual growth as it relates to God's power, growth in gratitude with respect to our Prophet illuminating the misery of our darkness, and growth in our King who enriches us by our participation in his kingdom. Let us now examine how the third office of Christ stirs our gratitude, and, in some respects, is the root of all.

Redemption, gratitude, and Christ our Priest

Colossians 1:14 brings us to the most fundamental blessing of redemption: the forgiveness of sins, on the ground of the satisfaction Christ made to God by the shedding of his blood on the cross. The word *redemption* means setting someone free from punishment or slavery by paying a price.[112] Without redemption, we have no comfort. Without redemption there can be no participation in the inheritance of the saints, no deliverance from the power of darkness, no translation into Christ's kingdom. Thankfully, redemption is ours as believers in Christ.

Our greatest need is redemption from the guilt of our sins. From earliest times it was understood that 'without shedding of blood' there can be no forgiveness of sins (Heb. 9:22). So under the law, Moses instituted a priesthood to offer sacrifices for the sins of the people. However, the Old Testament priesthood and the sacrifices offered by those priests were only 'a shadow of good things to come' (Heb. 10:1). 'For it is not possible that the blood of bulls and of goats should take away sins' (Heb. 10:4). In the fullness of time, God sent his Son into the world, 'made a high priest for ever after the order of Melchisedec' (Heb. 7:1; Ps. 110:4), to offer himself as the 'one sacrifice for sins for ever' (Heb. 10:12), by laying down his life at the cross. 'Once in the end of the world hath he appeared to put away sin by the sacrifice of himself' (Heb. 9:26).

With his precious blood, Christ has fully satisfied, or paid the debt of all our sins. The barrier that separated us from God has been taken away. The sins that estranged us from God have been wholly covered, so that we can be reconciled to him. The transgressions that kindled God's wrath against us, and brought down his curse upon us, have been purged away. How can we be sure? Because as our high priest, Christ rose from the dead and ascended into heaven, to present his crucified body and shed blood to God the Father, as the incontrovertible proof that the ransom has been paid, our sins have been purged, and the demands of God's justice have been satisfied for ever (Heb. 9:24-26).

Christ's offices of Prophet and King would be bad news for us if it were not for his office as Priest. Without this office, Christ's prophetic truth would only reveal our inevitable doom, and his kingly power would crush us as the enemies of God. But in his priestly office, Christ's sacrifice has secured God's grace and mercy for us. With Christ as our Priest, the words 'Forgiven, forgiven!' ring from heaven. Christ's truth and power sweetly come to heal us. As priest Christ has reconciled us to God and to each other 'in one body on the cross'. Now, as prophet, Christ promises us peace with God, and by the preaching of the gospel, beseeches us to be reconciled to God. As our king, he rules over all things, governing us by his Word and Spirit, defending us from our enemies and preserving us in the salvation he purchased for us.

Imagine the great day when the glory of Christ dawns over this world. The mighty men of the world who once strutted through the earth in pride will now cry out for the mountains to fall on them and hide them from the wrath of Christ. All monuments of man's workmanship will crack and crumble to the ground. Where will you go? God's eyes see everything; indeed, he knows your innermost thoughts and motives. You cannot hide from him.

But look! The Lord will smile upon his own people. They will be clothed in white, for they have been washed in the blood of the Lamb. O, how precious his blood will be on that great day! How grateful we will be if can say this King is also our Priest who has bought us with his blood. He has loved us and washed us from our sins with his own blood. O, thanks be to God for the blood of Christ! Worthy is the Lamb who is seated on the throne.

That should be our cry even today, for though the Lord tarries, we are rushing forward toward death. The wrath of God hangs over the world like the legendary sword of Damocles,[113] suspended by a thread. How precious then is the blood of Christ! How much more valuable it is than all the gold and silver that men possess! To have Christ as our redemption, Passover sacrifice, and only High Priest is everything, for he alone delivers us from the wrath of God and secures us in the love of God for ever.

The *Heidelberg Catechism* (Q. 1), said, 'What is thy only comfort in life and death? That I with body and soul, both in life and death, am not my own, but belong unto my faithful Savior Jesus Christ; who with His precious blood, hath fully satisfied for all my sins, and delivered me from all the power of the devil.'[114] If the root of our comfort is Christ's redemptive work, it is also the fuel for our gratitude. So the catechism adds these words: 'And thereby, by His Holy Spirit, He also assures me of eternal life, and makes me sincerely willing and ready, henceforth, to live unto Him.'[115]

The longer we live, striving against sin and seeking to please God, the more precious his sacrifice will appear in our eyes and the more grateful we shall be. Newton observed that for most of us, only after we have walked with God for some time do we have 'the most sensible and distressing experience of our evil natures'.[116] What he meant was, the longer we live, the more we learn to know our sinful nature, and to hate all sin with our whole heart.[117] Newton also said, 'The exceeding sinfulness of sin is manifested, not so much by its breaking through the restraint of threatening and commands, as by its being capable of acting against light and against love.'[118] As we grow spiritually, we become more horrified by how evil our hearts remain despite all that God has done for us.

So, as we walk with God, Christ's blood becomes ever more precious to us. Our gratitude also increases to his glory. Newton wrote: 'The repeated and multiplied pardons which the believer has received, increase his admiration of, and the sense of his obligations to, the rich sovereign abounding mercy of the covenant. Much has been forgiven him, therefore he loves much, and therefore he knows how to forgive and pity others.'[119] That is the experience of the growing believer, not the fresh convert.

Just as God redeemed Israel so they might serve him at Mount Sinai, so Christ redeemed his people to worship and serve God on earth and in heaven. The redeemed of the Lord 'as lively stones, are built up a spiritual house, an holy priesthood, to offer up spiritual sacrifices, acceptable to God by Jesus Christ' (1 Peter 2:4-6). These spiritual sacrifices are identified in Hebrews 13:15, as 'the sacrifice of praise', and 'the fruit of our lips giving thanks' to the name of God. Our great High Priest consecrates us as the temple of the living God, a house of prayer which God inhabits to receive the praises of his people. Gratitude is not an accidental effect of redemption. The purpose of God's eternal plan of redemption is that we might live in Christ to 'the praise of the glory of his grace' (Eph. 1:6). If this is God's purpose, we may be sure that the more Christ's blood is applied to our souls by knowing him, the more we will grow into living sacrifices and holy priests to the Lord.

Conclusion

Experiential knowledge of Christ is nothing less than the power of the gospel at work to transform lives. The Spirit's application of the gospel transforms fallen men by restoring them in the image and likeness of God. If we are want to resist false doctrine and spiritual decline, we must devote ourselves to knowing Christ, walking in Christ, and teaching others about Christ.

Calvin said, 'How comes it that we are "carried about with so many strange doctrines" (Heb. 13:9), but because the excellence of Christ is not perceived by us? For Christ alone makes all other things suddenly vanish… This, therefore, is the only means of retaining, as well as restoring pure doctrine — to place Christ before the view such as he is with all his blessings, that his excellence may be truly perceived.'[120]

Earlier I said that John Newton spoke of the mature stage of Christian growth as the period of 'contemplation'. That corresponds with 1 John 2:13a, which says, 'I write unto you, fathers, because ye have known him that is from the beginning.' Newton said the chief characteristic of a mature believer is that 'in the course of his experience, he has attained clearer, deeper, and more comprehensive views of the mystery of redeeming love; of the glorious excellency of the Lord Jesus… His great business is to behold the glory of God in Christ.'[121] As a result, 'The apprehension of infinite majesty combined with infinite love, makes him shrink into the dust' in humility; and there is 'a union of heart to the glory and will of God'.[122]

Christ's free grace is great enough to transform any life. In the early nineteenth century, an officer of the British army was involved in an unpleasant judicial case. Thomas Hutchens stood before that officer as a prisoner. Hutchens had been in military court many times before. He had been imprisoned, sentenced to hard labor, and flogged. Through it all he descended into darkness and his heart became hard. Now once again he was accused of a crime. Witnesses testified against him. When the officer asked him what he had to say in his defense, he replied, 'Nothing.' The officer then read aloud all the crimes that Hutchens was convicted of.

Then the officer did something shocking. He declared that the prisoner should be released to return to his duty. All the witnesses against him were dismissed. Furthermore, the officer said that Hutchens was from this time forth to be treated as a good soldier. People left the court in disbelief, leaving the officer with Hutchens. He said to Hutchens, 'My man, you see that you are free — go.'

The hardness in Thomas Hutchens melted. With tears pouring down his face, he confessed his sins, then promised he would change. The officer said, 'You are forgiven; go and sin no more.' Hutchens was never again jailed for misconduct. There is reason to believe that he became a Christian. His commanding officer remarked twenty-five years later that Hutchens became one of the best soldiers in his unit.[123]

When we hear that account, we are impressed by the transformation of a criminal into a loyal soldier. Yet we may find ourselves wondering if the officer took a tremendous risk in trusting Hutchens. Was his judgement fair? How could he let this wicked man go free? How could he trust him? Certainly these are legitimate questions to ask regarding human government, whether of civil or military authorities. But these same questions may also arise in our hearts towards God. Perhaps we question God's treatment of another sinner. Isn't God taking a terrible risk in adopting such a person as his child? Is it fair just to let such a sinner go free after all he has done?

Perhaps we ask such questions about ourselves. Why would God entrust me with responsibility in light of my sin that has only made me worthy of hell? How can he forgive me when I have been so stubbornly entrenched in wrong doing? Surely he would be right to withhold his blessing from the life, family and work of a sinner such as me.

When we find ourselves judging ourselves or others with secret doubts about the gospel's ability, we see how much more we need to know of the power of the gospel. We still have darkness inside of us that cries for greater illumination from our Prophet. We will see that nothing will break the hardened heart of man but the free grace of God. Christ is King, not only in promise but in experience. When God unites us to Christ in his kingdom, he creates not just a new position for us but also a new passion. And when God gives us redemption through Christ's blood — his agonizing, violent death on the cross — we realize that he is not unjust in setting sinners free, for Christ paid the debt of sin in full. An experiential knowledge of our Priest will not promote sin but godly sorrow in us, not rebellion but repentance, not a license to live as we please but the love to live for his pleasure.

Spiritual growth is a progressive experience of the all-sufficiency of Christ. The grace of our Lord Jesus Christ is sufficient to cover the entire Christian pilgrimage from conversion to glorification. No matter how great our sins are, Christ is greater. No matter how prolonged our trials, he will not leave us or forsake us. No matter how many or how great our needs are, God will supply them all out of his riches in Christ. His wisdom is greater than our foolishness. His power is greater than our weakness. His atonement is greater than our guilt.

So grow. By the Spirit's grace, grow in the grace of our Lord Jesus Christ.

Then ask God for more. Take Paul's prayer in Colossians 1 to heart and pray it regularly. Make these words your own: 'God and Father of our Lord Jesus Christ, I pray that I would be filled with the knowledge of Thy will in all wisdom and spiritual understanding, that I might walk worthy of my Lord unto all pleasing. By Thy grace let me become fruitful in every good work. Let me increase in the knowledge of God so that I am strengthened with all might, according to Thy glorious power, unto all patience and longsuffering with joyfulness; and giving thanks unto Thee, O Father, which hath made us meet to be partakers of the inheritance of the saints in light. Thou hast given me great reasons for thanksgiving, for Thou hast delivered me from the power of darkness, and hath translated me into the kingdom of Thy dear Son: in whom I have redemption through his blood, even the forgiveness of sins. Write these things on my heart.'

Aim high, then higher. George Whitefield (1714-1770) prayed: 'O Lord, make me an extraordinary Christian!'[124] Don't be satisfied with mediocrity. You are a child of the King. Pursue greatness as the servant of all for Christ's sake. Wisse wrote: 'The official ministry of Christ has no other purpose but the glorification of a triune God by His image-bearer, man. This glorification implies that the revelation of God and His most blessed attributes be responded to, be experienced, and be magnified in a manner commensurate with the grace that has been glorified. This means that the redeemed will one day be the flawless mirror in which God will see the reflection of His image.'[125] You who are the redeemed of the Lord have this destiny (Ps. 149). You cannot possibly aim too high or aspire to a goal too noble when God himself has created you to reflect his glory.

Be zealous. Work and pray for spiritual growth. There is no inconsistency between trusting in God's sovereignty and working with all your might, for it is God who works in you 'both to will and to do of his good pleasure' (Phil. 2:12-13).

Be patient as well, for spiritual growth is not a sprint but a marathon. Often growth is a slow, quiet process recognized only in retrospect. John Flavel said, 'Let us consider the growth of grace is discerned as the growth of plants is, which we perceive rather … to have grown than to grow.'[126] As you measure your growth, think in terms of years and decades, not days and weeks. Often the best way to recognize growth is to ask someone who has known you for a long time how they see God working in you.

Then, expect grace. If we are children of God, it is not arrogant to expect our Father to help us grow. The God of the covenant has plans for us for good and not evil, for a future and a hope. He has predestined us for glory in the likeness of his Son. May the hope of the gospel energize us to pursue Christ with all that we are.

Then, give thanks. Whenever you see evidence that God is growing you or someone else, even the smallest way, give glory to the Lord. God's purpose is to turn all things to his glory, so cooperate with him. Too many Christians view their cups as half-empty in regard to their spiritual growth. Yes, we continue to fall into sin even after conversion. That should not lead us to despair of God's grace. The holiest men may have only a beginning of holiness, but a beginning is a beginning, nonetheless. The depravity of our nature notwithstanding, shouldn't we rejoice at every drop of the Holy Spirit that falls into our lives? Give thanks for growth, and you will grow the more.

Finally, live as Christ's willing *doulos* — this is, as Christ's willing servant or slave. That servitude is beautifully illustrated in the nineteenth-century story of a young African woman who was being sold one day in New Orleans when a wealthy English nobleman, standing in back of the crowd, offered to pay twice the amount anyone else would pay for this slave. The auctioneer was astonished. 'No one has ever paid this much for a slave,' he said. 'Do you really have the money?' When the nobleman waved the bills, the auctioneer said, 'Sold!'

As the nobleman gave the young woman a hand to help her down from the stand, she spat him in the face. He wiped the spit away and took her by the hand to an office, where he signed her manumission papers and handed them to her. Again she spat him in the face. He wiped the spit away, and said, 'Don't you understand? You are free!'

The woman stared at him, then collapsed at his feet, and began to cry. After crying for some time, she looked up and said, 'Do you mean to tell me that you paid twice the amount that anyone has ever paid for the price of a slave just to set me free?'

'Yes,' he said. And she wept some more.

Finally, she looked up at him and said, 'Sir, I have just one favor to ask of you: can I be your slave for ever?'

That is precisely how true Christians feel when we are set free by Christ's blood after repeatedly spitting him in the face with our sins and rebellion. We then want to serve him as willing slaves — for ever. The more the spirit of a willing *doulos* consumes us, the greater our spiritual growth is.

Notes

1. On the city of Colossae, see Peter T. O'Brien, *Colossians, Philemon,* Word Biblical Commentary, Vol. 44 (Nashville: Thomas Nelson, 1982), xxvi.

2. Quoted in John Blanchard, *The Complete Gathered Gold* (Darlington, Eng.: Evangelical Press, 2006), 277.

3. Wilhelmus á Brakel, *The Christian's Reasonable Service,* trans. Bartel Elshout, ed. Joel R. Beeke (Grand Rapids: Reformation Heritage Books, 1999), 3:139-40.

4. Gardiner Spring, *The Distinguishing Traits of Christian Character* (Philadelphia: Presbyterian & Reformed, 1967), 65.

5. E.g. Rom. 15:13; Eph. 1:15-20; 3:14-21; Phil. 1:9-11; 1 Thess. 3:11-13; 2 Thess. 1:11-12; 3:5.

6. Robert Rollock, *Lectvres Vpon the Epistle of Pavl to the Colossians* (London: Felix Kyngston, 1603), 16.

7. Col. 1:9, 19, 24, 25; 2:2, 9, 10; 4:12; *cf.* Eph. 1:10, 23; 3:19; 4:10, 13; 5:18.

8. Rollock, *Colossians,* 17.

9. John Angell James, *Christian Progress* (New York: American Tract Society, [1854]), 54.

10. Curtis Vaughan, *Expositor's Bible Commentary,* Zondervan Reference Software (Grand Rapids: Zondervan, 1998), comm. Col. 1:19.

11. *Heidelberg Catechism,* Q. 31.

12. *Matthew Henry's Commentary on the Whole Bible* (Peabody, Mass.: Hendrickson, 1991), 4:943 [on Hos. 14:4-7].

13. John Davenant, *An Exposition of the Epistle of St. Paul to the Colossians* (London: Hamilton, Adams, and Co., 1831), 1:122.

14. John Calvin, *Commentary on the Epistle to the Colossians* (repr., Grand Rapids: Baker, 1996), 144.

15. 'The Excellency of Christ', in *The Works of John Owen* (1850-1853; repr., Edinburgh: Banner of Truth, 1998), 9:475.

16. *The Works of the Late Rev. Robert Murray M'Cheyne* (New York: Robert Carter, 1847), 2:287.

17. Jerry Bridges, *Growing Your Faith* (Colorado Springs: NavPress, 2004), 18.

18. Bridges, *Growing Your Faith,* 20-23.

19. 'Christ Our Mediator,' in *The Works of Thomas Goodwin, Volume 5* (Grand Rapids: Reformation Heritage Books, 2006); Isaac Ambrose, *Looking unto Jesus* (Harrisonburg, Va.: Sprinkle Publications, 1988); Ralph Robinson, *Christ All and in All* (Ligonier, Pa.: Soli Deo Gloria, 1992); Philip Henry, *Christ All in All* (Swengel, Pa.: Reiner, 1976); John Brown, *Christ: the Way, the Truth, and the Life* (Morgan, Pa.: Soli Deo Gloria, 1995); 'A Declaration of the Glorious Mystery of the Person of Christ,' in *The Works of John Owen, Volume 1* (Edinburgh: Banner of Truth, 1965); James Durham, *Christ Crucified* (Dallas: Naphtali Press, 2001).

20. *Heidelberg Catechism,* Q. 1, quoted in *Doctrinal Standards, Liturgy, and Church Order* (Grand Rapids: Reformation Heritage Books, 2003), 27.

21. John Eadie, *Colossians* (1856; repr. Minneapolis: Klock & Klock, 1980), 24.

22. John Calvin, *Institutes of the Christian Religion,* ed. John T. McNeill, trans. Ford Lewis Battles (Philadelphia: Westminster Press, 1960), 1.2.1. For a comparison of the views of the authors of the *Heidelberg Catechism* on faith and knowledge to the view of Calvin, see Joel R. Beeke, 'Faith and Assurance in the Heidelberg Catechism and Its Primary Composers: A Fresh Look at the Kendall Thesis', *Calvin Theological Journal* 27, no. 1 (Apr. 1992): 39-67.

23. In the Greek text 'walk' is an infinitive (περιπατησαι), indicating the result or purpose of the verb 'be filled'.

24. Quoted in James M. Boice and Philip Graham Ryken, *The Doctrines of Grace: Rediscovering the Evangelical Gospel* (Wheaton: Crossway, 2002), 179.

25. *Selected Spiritual Writings of Anne Dutton, Volume 3, The Autobiography,* ed. JoAnn Ford Watson (Macon, Ga.: Mercer University Press, 2006), 120.

26. Quoted in Blanchard, *The Complete Gathered Gold,* 278.

27. Paul Baynes, *A Commentarie Vpon the First and Second Chapters of Saint Paul to the Colossians* (London: by Richard Badger, for Nicholas Bourne, 1635), 36.

28. E.g. 1 Cor. 8:6; Eph. 1:2, 3, 17; 5:20; 6:23; Phil. 2:11; Col. 1:2, 3; 3:17; and many others.

29. Joel R. Beeke, *Heirs with Christ: The Puritans on Adoption* (Grand Rapids: Reformation Heritage Books, 2008), 79-89.

30. *Heidelberg Catechism,* Q. 42.

31. Eadie, *Colossians,* 27.

32. Beeke, ed., *Doctrinal Standards,* 6.

33. Stephen Charnock, *The Existence and Attributes of God* (Grand Rapids: Baker, 1979); William Bates, *The Harmony of the Divine Attributes in the Contrivance and Accomplishment of Redemption* (Harrisonburg, Va.: Sprinkle, 1985); Edward H. Bickersteth, *The Trinity* (Grand Rapids: Kregel, 1965); Robert Letham, *The Holy Trinity In Scripture, History, Theology, and Worship*

(Phillipsburg, N.J.: P&R, 2004).

34. Nicholas Byfield, *Colossians* (Edinburgh: James Nichol, 1869), 88.

35. The actual phrase reads in Latin, 'Qui cessat esse melior, cessat esse bonus.' *The Journal of the British Archaeological Association,* vol. 13 (London: J. R. Smith and G. Wright, 1857), 344.

36. Num. 32:12; Deut. 1:36; Josh. 14:8, 9, 14.

37. Quoted in Blanchard, *The Complete Gathered Gold*, 277.

38. Quoted in Blanchard, *The Complete Gathered Gold,* 278.

39. Beeke, ed., *Doctrinal Standards,* 81.

40. Davenant, *Colossians,* 122.

41. The Greek adverb is αξιως.

42. See Davenant, *Colossians,* 124. The Greek adjective in Matt. 3:8 is αξιος.

43. Eadie, *Colossians,* 25.

44. Thomas Watson, *A Body of Practical Divinity* (London: A. Fullarton, 1845), 182.

45. J. I. Packer, *Rediscovering Holiness* (Ann Arbor, Mich.: Servant Publications, 1992), 120–21.

46. Beeke, ed., *Doctrinal Standards,* 85.

47. E.g. Rom. 13:1-7; Eph. 5:21 – 6:9; Titus 3:1-2.

48. Greek διακονος.

49. 2 Cor. 1:5; 4:10; Phil. 3:10; Col. 1:24.

50. John Calvin, *Golden Booklet of the Christian Life,* trans. Henry J. Van Andel (Grand Rapids: Baker, 2004), 23. See John Calvin, *Institutes of the Christian Religion,* trans. Ford Lewis Battles, ed. John T. McNeill (Philadelphia: Westminster, 1960), 3.7.5.

51. Gal. 1:10; 2 Cor. 5:9; 2 Tim. 2:4.

52. Calvin, *Commentary on the Epistle to the Colossians,* 144.

53. Byfield, *Colossians,* 84.

54. Beeke, ed., *Doctrinal Standards,* 16.

55. Davenant, *Colossians,* 126.

56. Davenant, *Colossians,* 126–27.

57. Greek καρποφορουμενον.

58. Portions of the following section are adapted from Joel R. Beeke, *Living for God's Glory: An Introduction to Calvinism* (Orlando: Reformation Trust, 2008), 204-212, 337-43.

59. The sacraments of baptism and the Lord's Supper are included as 'visible words' under the Word.

60. Austin Phelps, *The Still Hour, or Communion with God* (Boston: Gould and Lincoln, 1860), 93-94.

61. *Westminster Confession of Faith* (Glasgow: Free Presbyterian Publications, 2003), 249-50.

62. Archibald Alexander, *Thoughts on Religious Experience* (London: Banner of Truth, 1967), 162.

63. E.g. Exod. 13:3, 8-10; Deut. 32:7; Ps. 78:1-8; 111:2-4.

64. For more details on this important family discipline, see Joel R. Beeke, *Family Worship* (Grand Rapids: Reformation Heritage Books, 2009).

65. 'Form for the Administration of the Lord's Supper,' *The Psalter,* 138.

66. 'Form for the Lord's Supper,' *Psalter,* 139.

67. *Larger Catechism,* Q. 167.

68. *Larger Catechism,* Q. 170-175.

69. Wilhelmus à Brakel, *The Christian's Reasonable Service* (Grand Rapids: Reformation Heritage Books, 2011), vol. 2, ch. 41.

70. R. Kent Hughes, *Colossians and Philemon: The Supremacy of Christ* (Westchester, Ill.: Crossway, 1989), 25.

71. David P. Murray, 'What happened to Evangelistic Preaching?' http://s3.amazonaws.com/files.posterous.com/headheartha nd/55R2oyvjS16fwHEclJUqm5MsgyssVzywLg8BUkHlw0 ky9Cg7s5Wacxd3QELX/Evangelistic_Preaching.pdf?AWS AccessKeyId=AKIAJFZAE65UYRT34AOQ&Expires=13 18015848&Signature=jMcXHJcJYivk8qtCzA7kSInqzPc% 3D (accessed October 7, 2011).

72. Alexander, *Thoughts on Religious Experience,* 166.

73. Thomas Scott, 'A Treatise on Growth in Grace', in *Treatises on Various Theological Subjects* (Middletown, Conn.: Clark and Lyman, 1815), 161.

74. Scott, 'A Treatise on Growth in Grace', in *Treatises,* 161.

75. Thomas Cartwright, *A Commentary upon the Epistle of St Paul Written to the Colossians* (Edinburgh: James Nichol, 1864), 12. This is bound with Henry Airay, *Lectures upon the Whole Epistle of St Paul to the Philippians.*

76. R. C. Sproul, *Five Things Every Christian Needs to Grow* (Orlando: Reformation Trust, 2008), 91.

77. *The Works of the Late Rev. Robert Murray M'Cheyne* (New York: Robert Carter, 1847), 2:470.

78. 'Grace Abounding to the Chief of Sinners', sec. 37, 38, in *The Works of John Bunyan,* ed. George Offor (Glasgow: Blackie and Son, 1855), 1:10.

79. *The Works of the Rev. John Newton* (New York: Williams & Whiting, 1810), 1:184.

80. Davenant, *An Exposition of the Epistle of St. Paul to the Colossians,* 132.

81. Davenant, *An Exposition of the Epistle of St. Paul to the Colossians,* 134.

82. *Heidelberg Catechism*, Q. 32.

83. Davenant, *An Exposition of the Epistle of St. Paul to the Colossians,* 134.

84. Newton, *Works,* 1:185. Newton referred to the different stages of the Christian life as A, B, and C.

85. Greek υπομονη. E.g. Luke 8:15; Rom. 2:7; 2 Cor. 1:6; 6:4; 2 Thess. 1:4; Heb. 10:36; 12:1. See O'Brien, *Colossians and Philemon,* 24.

86. Greek μακροθυμια. E.g. Rom. 2:4; Eph. 4:2; Col. 3:12; 1 Tim. 1:16; *cf.* μακροθυμος in LXX Ex. 34:6.

87. Beeke, ed., *Doctrinal Standards,* 68.

88. Darlene Deibler Rose, *Evidence Not Seen: A Woman's*

Miraculous Faith in the Jungles of World War II (San Francisco: Harper Collins, 1988), ix, 121ff, 141-42. The song is by Annie Johnson Flint.

89. Though some interpreters have seen this verse as a continuation of Paul's thanksgivings and prayers begun in verses 3, 9, and others as the beginning of a new section confessing faith in Christ (vv. 12-20), it is better to take it alongside the previous three participial phrases of verses 10-11 as a continuing description of the kind of spiritual growth for which Paul prayed. So Eadie, *Colossians,* 31; O'Brien, *Colossians and Philemon,* 19-20.

90. The Greek words for thanksgiving (ευχαριστια) and grace (χαρις) are directly related.

91. The word translated 'thanks' is the same word translated 'grace' (χαρις) in previous verses.

92. *Belgic Confession,* Art. 1.

93. Owen, 'Communion with God', in *Works,* 2:24.

94. 'Made us meet' (ικανοω) is a verb that can connote ability/ sufficiency (2 Cor. 3:5-6) or worthiness (*cf.* ικανος in Matt. 3:11; 1 Cor. 15:9). In this context it evidently refers to granting the right of an heir to the 'inheritance'.

95. The noun (ικανος) cognate to the verb translated 'made us meet' is 'used in the LXX at Job 31:2 as a divine name, "the Almighty",' and some have suggested that this title of God influenced Paul here in describing God's mighty work of redeeming sinners (O'Brien, *Colossians and Philemon,* 25).

96. Gerard Wisse, *Christ's Ministry in the Christian,* trans. Bartel Elshout and William Van Voorst (Sioux Center, Iowa: Netherland Reformed Book and Publishing, 1993), 4-5.

97. Greek εξουσια.

98. Wisse, *Christ's Ministry in the Christian,* 11.

99. The verb is *metestesen,* a word that was used in secular literature in reference to 'removing persons from one country and

settling them as colonists and citizens in another country.'
Vaughan, in *Expositor's Bible Commentary,* comm. Col. 1:12.
See also Davenant, *An Exposition of the Epistle of St. Paul to the Colossians,* 158.

100. Wisse, *Christ's Ministry in the Christian,* 80.

101. Wisse, *Christ's Ministry in the Christian,* 82.

102. Wisse, *Christ's Ministry in the Christian,* 92.

103. Davenant, *An Exposition of the Epistle of St. Paul to the Colossians,* 160.

104. Owen, 'Communion with God', in *Works,* 2:137.

105. The phrase 'the Son of his love' (του υιου της αγαπης αυτου) is *hapax legomenon* in the Greek Bible. Similar phrases appear of Abraham's love for Isaac (LXX Gen. 22:2, 12, 16), God's love for Ephraim (LXX Jer. 38[31]:20), and the Father's love for Jesus (Matt. 3:17; 17:5; Mark 1:11; 9:7; 12:6; Luke 3:22; 20:13; 2 Peter 1:17; *cf.* Eph. 1:6).

106. Eadie, *Colossians,* 38.

107. Beeke, *Living for God's Glory,* 256. Elements of the following section are drawn from chapter 19 of this book.

108. Beeke, *Living for God's Glory,* 258.

109. Robert Burns, introduction to *Works of Thomas Halyburton* (London: Thomas Tegg, 1835), xv.

110. 'The Directory for the Publick Worship of God', in *Westminster Confession of Faith,* 380.

111. 'Form for the Administration of Baptism', *The Psalter,* 127.

112. LXX Exod. 21:30; Lev. 25:47-55.

113. Damocles lived in ancient Sicily under the rule of Dionysius the Elder. When Damocles extolled the power and wealth of Dionysius, the tyrant invited him to a state dinner as guest of honor, so that he could experience for himself what it was to rule over such a kingdom. Damocles was seated at the table, and began to enjoy himself to the full, until he looked up and saw a great sword suspended by a single horse hair, ready

to fall on him at any moment. The lesson for Damocles was, however wealthy and powerful Dionysius was, he lived every moment in peril of his life, because of his many enemies.

114. Beeke, ed., *Doctrinal Standards,* 27.

115. Beeke, ed., *Doctrinal Standards,* 27.

116. Newton, *Works,* 1:182.

117. *Heidelberg Catechism*, QQ. 113, 115.

118. Newton, *Works,* 1:181.

119. Newton, *Works,* 1:183.

120. Calvin, *Commentary on the Epistle to the Colossians,* 146.

121. Newton, *Works,* 1:186.

122. Newton, *Works,* 1:186, 188.

123. 'The Pardoned Criminal', in *The British Evangelist* 1, no. 1 (January 1, 1869): 7.

124. Blanchard, *The Complete Gathered Gold,* 692.

125. Wisse, *Christ's Ministry in the Christian,* 94.

126. *The Whole Works of the Rev. Mr. John Flavel* (London: W. Baynes and Son, 1820), 5:572.